THE
DAILY
BIBLE

THE
DAILY BIBLE

SELECTIONS FROM THE
NEW INTERNATIONAL VERSION

Scripture Union
130 City Road, London EC1V 2NJ

© Scripture Union 1980
First published 1980 by Ark Publishing,
130 City Road, London EC1V 2NJ

This edition published 1981
Reprinted 1984

Selections by Rev. Michael Perry

From the New International Version of the Bible
© UK 1979 by the New York International
Bible Society and used by permission.

ISBN 0 86201 124 8

Phototypeset by Input Typesetting Ltd., London SW19.
Printed and bound in Great Britain by
William Clowes Limited, Beccles and London

Foreword

The readings in *The Daily Bible* have been arranged in three ways.

First: the book has been divided into thirty-four sections. These sections have been designed to reflect not only the generally accepted pattern of the Christian year, but also the main themes of life and faith. By using the Contents page, Bible study groups and leaders may gain access to the Bible's collected teaching.

Second: each day's material gives the reader a number of passages which match and complement each other, in order to give a deeper understanding of each day's subject.

Third: the Bible passages have been set in lines of speech-equivalence, to make understanding easier and to facilitate reading out loud in group studies.

As a result, *The Daily Bible* is more than a regular devotional manual; it is also a source book for study and a ready reference to Christian teaching.

MICHAEL PERRY

Contents

God chooses the times

There is a time for everything,
and a season for every activity under heaven:
a time to be born and a time to die,
a time to plant and a time to uproot,
a time to kill and a time to heal,
a time to tear down and a time to build,
a time to weep and a time to laugh,
a time to mourn and a time to dance,
a time to scatter stones and a time to gather them,
a time to embrace and a time to refrain,
a time to search and a time to give up,
a time to keep and a time to throw away,
a time to tear and a time to mend,
a time to be silent and a time to speak,
a time to love and a time to hate,
a time for war and a time for peace.   ECCLESIASTES 3:1–8

So when the apostles met together,
they asked Jesus,
'Lord, are you at this time going to restore
the kingdom to Israel?'
He said to them:
'It is not for you to know the times or dates
the Father has set by his own authority.'   ACTS 1:6,7

Eternal God, mortal man

Lord, you have been our dwelling-place
    throughout all generations.
Before the mountains were born
or you brought forth the earth and the world,
from everlasting to everlasting you are God.
You turn men back to dust, saying,
'Return to dust, O sons of men.'
For a thousand years in your sight
are like a day that has just gone by,
or like a watch in the night.
You sweep men away in the sleep of death;
they are like the new grass of the morning –
though in the morning it springs up new,
by evening it is dry and withered.   PSALM 90:1–6

Now there was a man in Jerusalem called Simeon,
who was righteous and devout.
He was waiting for the consolation of Israel,
and the Holy Spirit was upon him.
It had been revealed to him by the Holy Spirit
that he would not die
before he had seen the Lord's Christ.
Moved by the Spirit, he went into the temple courts.
When the parents brought in the child Jesus
to do for him what the custom of the Law required,
Simeon took him in his arms and praised God, saying:
'Sovereign Lord, as you have promised,
you now dismiss your servant in peace.'   LUKE 2:25–29

The God of time and eternity

My days are swifter than a runner;
they fly away without a glimpse of joy.
They skim past like boats of papyrus,
like eagles swooping down on their prey.
If I say, 'I will forget my complaint,
I will change my expression, and smile,'
I still dread all my sufferings,
for I know you will not hold me innocent.   JOB 9:25–28

I said, 'I will watch my ways
and keep my tongue from sin;
I will put a muzzle on my mouth
as long as the wicked are in my presence.'
But when I was silent and still,
not even saying anything good,
my anguish increased.
My heart grew hot within me,
and as I meditated, the fire burned;
then I spoke with my tongue:
'Show me, O Lord, my life's end
     and the number of my days;
let me know how fleeting is my life.
You have made my days a mere handbreadth;
the span of my years is as nothing before you.
Each man's life is but a breath.'   PSALM 39:1–5

Then man goes to his eternal home
and mourners go about the streets.
Remember him – before the silver cord is severed,
or the golden bowl is broken;
before the pitcher is shattered at the spring,
or the wheel broken at the well,
and the dust returns to the ground it came from,
and the spirit returns to God who gave it.
    ECCLESIASTES 12:5,6,7

The God of wisdom

If any of you lacks wisdom,
he should ask God,
who gives generously to all
      without finding fault;
and it will be given to him.   JAMES 1:5

Does not wisdom call out?
Does not understanding raise her voice?
On the heights along the way,
where the paths meet, she takes her stand;
beside the gates leading into the city,
at the entrances, she cries aloud:
'To you, O men, I call out;
I raise my voice to all mankind.
You who are simple, gain prudence;
you who are foolish, gain understanding.
Listen, for I have worthy things to say;
I open my lips to speak what is right.
My mouth speaks what is true,
for my lips detest wickedness.
All the words of my mouth are just;
none of them is crooked or perverse.
To the discerning all of them are right;
they are faultless to those who have knowledge.
Choose my instruction instead of silver,
knowledge rather than choice gold.'   PROVERBS 8:1–10

The fear of the Lord is the beginning of wisdom,
and knowledge of the Holy One is understanding.
For through me your days will be many,
and years will be added to your life.
If you are wise, your wisdom will reward you;
if you are a mocker, you alone will suffer.

                                              PROVERBS 9:10–12

God's wisdom is different from ours

Who has understood the Spirit of the Lord,
or instructed him as his counsellor?
Whom did the Lord consult to enlighten him,
and who taught him the right way?
'For my thoughts are not your thoughts,
neither are your ways my ways,'
        declares the Lord.
'As the heavens are higher than the earth,
so are my ways higher than your ways
and my thoughts than your thoughts.'   ISAIAH 40:13,14 55:8,9

For since in the wisdom of God
the world through its wisdom did not know him,
God was pleased through the foolishness
        of what was preached
to save those who believe.
For the foolishness of God
        is wiser than man's wisdom,
and the weakness of God
        is stronger than man's strength.   1 CORINTHIANS 1:21,25

Oh, the depth of the riches of the wisdom
        and knowledge of God!
How unsearchable his judgements,
and his paths beyond tracing out!
For from him and through him
        and to him are all things.
To him be the glory for ever! Amen.   ROMANS 12:33,36

Wisdom is hidden in Christ

The words of the wise are like goads,
their collected sayings like firmly embedded nails –
given by one Shepherd.   ECCLESIASTES 12:11

Wisdom is supreme; therefore get wisdom.
Though it cost all you have, get understanding.
Esteem her, and she will exalt you;
embrace her, and she will honour you.
She will set a garland of grace on your head
and present you with a crown of splendour.
When you walk, your steps will not be hampered;
when you run, you will not stumble.
Hold on to instruction, do not let it go;
guard it well, for it is your life.   PROVERBS 4:7–9,12,13

My purpose is that they may be encouraged in heart
and united in love,
so that they may have the full riches
     of complete understanding,
in order that they may know the mystery of God,
     namely, Christ,
in whom are hidden
all the treasures of wisdom and knowledge.   COLOSSIANS 2:2,3

It is because of God
that you are in Christ Jesus,
who has become for us wisdom from God –
that is, our righteousness,
     holiness and redemption.
Therefore, as it is written:
'Let him who boasts boast in the Lord.'
                              1 CORINTHIANS 1:30,31

Wisdom is more valuable than wealth

God said to Solomon,
'Since this is your heart's desire
and you have not asked for wealth, riches or honour,
nor for the death of your enemies,
and since you have not asked for a long life
but for wisdom and knowledge to govern my people
      over whom I have made you king,
therefore wisdom and knowledge will be given you.
And I will also give you wealth, riches and honour,
such as no king who was before you ever had
and none after you will have.'   2 CHRONICLES 1:11,12

But where can wisdom be found?
Where does understanding dwell?
It cannot be bought with the finest gold,
nor can its price be weighed in silver.
It cannot be bought with the gold of Ophir,
with precious onyx or sapphires.
Neither gold nor crystal can compare with it,
nor can it be had for jewels of gold.
Coral and jasper are not worthy of mention;
the price of wisdom is beyond rubies.
The topaz of Cush cannot compare with it;
it cannot be bought with pure gold.
God understands the way to it
and he alone knows where it dwells,
for he views the ends of the earth
and sees everything under the heavens.
And he said to man,
'The fear of the Lord – that is wisdom,
and to shun evil is understanding.'   JOB 28:12,15–19,23,24,28

The holiness of God

The word of the Lord came to Ezekiel the priest . . .
the hand of the Lord was upon him.
I looked, and I saw a windstorm
    coming out of the north –
an immense cloud with flashing lightning
and surrounded by brilliant light.
The centre of the fire looked like glowing metal.

EZEKIEL 1:3,4

I saw the Lord seated on a throne,
high and exalted,
and the train of his robe filled the temple.
Above him were seraphs,
each with six wings:
with two wings they covered their faces,
with two they covered their feet,
and with two they were flying.
And they were calling to one another:
'Holy, holy, holy is the Lord Almighty;
the whole earth is full of his glory.'

ISAIAH 6:1–3

Day and night they never stop saying:
'Holy, holy, holy is the Lord God Almighty,
who was, and is, and is to come.'
The living creatures
give glory, honour and thanks
to him who sits on the throne
and who lives for ever and ever.

REVELATION 4:8,9

The majesty of God

David praised the Lord
in the presence of the whole assembly,
saying,
'Praise be to you, O Lord, God of our father Israel,
from everlasting to everlasting.
Yours, O Lord, is the greatness and the power
and the glory and the majesty and the splendour,
for everything in heaven and earth is yours.
Yours, O Lord, is the kingdom;
you are exalted as head over all.
Wealth and honour come from you;
you are the ruler of all things.
In your hands are strength and power
to exalt and give strength to all.
Now, our God, we give you thanks,
and praise your glorious name.'   1 CHRONICLES 29:10–13

They held harps given them by God
and sang. . .
'Great and marvellous are your deeds,
     Lord God Almighty.
Just and true are your ways,
     King of the ages.
Who will not fear you, O Lord,
and bring glory to your name?
For you alone are holy.
All nations will come and worship before you,
for your righteous acts have been revealed.'
                         REVELATION 15:2,3,4

The glory of God

While Aaron was speaking
to the whole Israelite community,
they looked towards the desert,
and there was the glory of the Lord
    appearing in the cloud.   EXODUS 16:10

Mount Sinai was covered with smoke,
because the Lord descended on it in fire. . .
Moses went up and the Lord said to him,
'Go down and warn the people
so they do not force their way through
    to see the Lord
and many of them perish.'   EXODUS 19:18,21

Now the ministry that brought death,
which was engraved in letters on stone,
came with glory,
so that the Israelites could not look
    steadily at the face of Moses
because of its glory.   2 CORINTHIANS 3:7

Jesus took Peter, John and James with him
and went up onto a mountain to pray.
As he was praying,
the appearance of his face changed,
and his clothes became as bright
    as a flash of lightning.
Two men, Moses and Elijah,
appeared in glorious splendour,
talking with Jesus.   LUKE 9:28–31

The wonder of God's glory

The heavens declare the glory of God;
the skies proclaim the work of his hands.
Day after day they pour forth speech;
night after night they display knowledge.
There is no speech or language
where their voice is not heard.
Their voice goes out into all the earth,
their words to the ends of the world.
In the heavens he has pitched a tent for the sun,
which is like a bridegroom coming forth
    from his pavilion,
like a champion rejoicing to run his course.   PSALM 19:1–5

Now no-one can look at the sun,
bright as it is in the skies
    after the wind has swept them clean.
Out of the north he comes in golden splendour;
God comes in awesome majesty.
The Almighty is beyond our reach
and exalted in power;
in his justice and great righteousness
he does not oppress.
Therefore, men revere him.   JOB 37:21-23,24

For God, who said,
'Let light shine out of darkness,'
made his light shine in our hearts
to give us the light of the knowledge
    of the glory of God
in the face of Christ.   2 CORINTHIANS 4:6

God the creator

In the beginning
you laid the foundations of the earth,
and the heavens are the work of your hands.
They will perish, but you remain;
they will all wear out like a garment.
Like clothing you will change them
   and they will be discarded.
But you remain the same,
and your years will never end.   PSALM 102:25–27

In the beginning
God created the heavens and the earth.
Now the earth was formless and empty,
darkness was over the surface of the deep,
and the Spirit of God was hovering over the waters.
And God said, 'Let there be light,'
and there was light...
And there was evening, and there was morning –
the first day.   GENESIS 1:1–3,5

Praise the Lord from the heavens,
praise him in the heights above.
Praise him, sun and moon,
praise him, all you shining stars.
Let them praise the name of the Lord,
for he commanded and they were created.
He set them in place for ever and ever;
he gave a decree that will never pass away.   PSALM 148:1,3,5,6

God the giver of everything

How many are your works, O Lord!
In wisdom you made them all;
the earth is full of your creatures.
These all look to you
     to give them their food at the proper time.
When you give it to them, they gather it up;
when you open your hand,
they are satisfied with good things.
When you hide your face, they are terrified;
when you take away their breath,
they die and return to the dust.
When you send your Spirit, they are created,
and you renew the face of the earth.   PSALM 104:24,27–30

And the Lord God formed man
     from the dust of the ground
and breathed into his nostrils the breath of life,
and man became a living being.   GENESIS 2:7

The God who made the world and everything in it
is the Lord of heaven and earth
and does not live in temples built by hands.
And he is not served by human hands,
as if he needed anything,
because he himself gives all men life and breath
     and everything else...
He is not far from each one of us.
'For in him we live and move and have our being.'
    ACTS 17:24,25,27,28

How small man is!

Your hands shaped me and made me.
Will you now turn and destroy me?
Remember that you moulded me like clay.
Will you now turn me to dust again?
Did you not pour me out like milk
and curdle me like cheese,
clothe me with skin and flesh
and knit me together with bones and sinews?
You gave me life and showed me kindness,
and in your providence watched over my spirit.   JOB 10:8–12

Who are you, O man,
to talk back to God?
'Shall what is formed
say to him who formed it,
"Why did you make me like this?" '
Does not the potter have the right
     to make out of the same lump of clay
some pottery for noble purposes
and some for common use?   ROMANS 9:20,21

I went down to the potter's house,
and I saw him working at the wheel.
But the pot he was shaping from the clay
was marred in his hands;
so the potter formed it into another pot,
shaping it as seemed best to him.
Then the word of the Lord came to me:
'O house of Israel, can I not do with you
     as this potter does?'
declares the Lord.
'Like clay in the hand of the potter,
so are you in my hand, O house of Israel.'

          JEREMIAH 18:3–6

The anointed Jesus

Here is my servant, whom I uphold,
my chosen one in whom I delight;
I will put my Spirit on him
and he will bring justice to the nations.
He will not shout or cry out,
or raise his voice in the streets.
A bruised reed he will not break,
and a smouldering wick he will not snuff out.
In faithfulness he will bring forth justice;
he will not falter or be discouraged
till he establishes justice on earth.
In his law the islands will put their hope.   ISAIAH 42:1–4

Jesus returned to Galilee in the power of the Spirit,
and news about him spread through the whole countryside.
He went to Nazareth, where he had been brought up,
and on the Sabbath day he went into the synagogue,
        as was his custom.
And he stood up to read.
The scroll of the prophet Isaiah was handed to him.
Unrolling it, he found the place where it is written:
'The Spirit of the Lord is on me,
because he has anointed me to preach good news
        to the poor.
He has sent me to proclaim freedom for the prisoners
and recovery of sight for the blind,
to release the oppressed,
to proclaim the year of the Lord's favour.'   LUKE 4:14,16–19

The bringer of good news

When John heard in prison what Christ was doing,
he sent his disciples to ask him,
'Are you the one who was to come,
or should we expect someone else?'
Jesus replied, 'Go back and report to John
      what you hear and see:
The blind receive sight, the lame walk,
those who have leprosy are cured,
the deaf hear, the dead are raised,
and the good news is preached to the poor.
Blessed is the man who does not fall away
      on account of me.'   MATTHEW 11:2–6

Strengthen the feeble hands,
steady the knees that give way;
say to those with fearful hearts,
'Be strong, do not fear;
your God will come, he will come with vengeance;
with divine retribution he will come to save you.'
Then will the eyes of the blind be opened
and the ears of the deaf unstopped.
Then will the lame leap like a deer,
and the tongue of the dumb shout for joy.
Water will gush forth in the wilderness
and streams in the desert.
And a highway will be there;
it will be called the Way of Holiness.
The unclean will not journey on it;
it will be for those who walk in that Way;
wicked fools will not go about on it.   ISAIAH 35:3–6,8

Jesus' love of children

Jesus took a little child
and had him stand among them.
Taking him in his arms,
he said to them,
'Whoever welcomes one of these little children
    in my name
welcomes me;
and whoever welcomes me
does not welcome me
but the one who sent me.'   MARK 9:36,37

If anyone causes
one of these little ones who believe in me
to sin,
it would be better for him
to be thrown into the sea
with a large millstone tied around his neck.   MARK 9:42

Jesus said to them,
'Let the little children come to me,
and do not hinder them,
for the kingdom of God belongs to such as these.
I tell you the truth,
anyone who will not receive the kingdom of God
like a little child
will never enter it.'
And he took the children in his arms,
put his hands on them and blessed them.   MARK 10:14–16

Jesus' teaching on responsibility

In reply Jesus said:
'A man was going down from Jerusalem to Jericho,
when he fell into the hands of robbers.
They stripped him of his clothes,
beat him and went away, leaving him half-dead.
A priest happened to be going down the same road,
and when he saw the man,
he passed by on the other side.
So too, a Levite,
when he came to the place and saw him,
passed by on the other side.
But a Samaritan, as he travelled,
came where the man was;
and when he saw him, he took pity on him.
He went to him and bandaged his wounds,
pouring on oil and wine.
Then he put the man on his own donkey,
brought him to an inn and took care of him.
Which of these three do you think
was a neighbour to the man
who fell into the hands of robbers?'
The expert in the law replied,
'The one who had mercy on him.'
Jesus told him, 'Go and do likewise.'   LUKE 10:30–34,36,37

If you lend to those from whom you expect repayment,
what credit is that to you?
Even 'sinners' lend to 'sinners',
expecting to be repaid in full.
But love your enemies, do good to them,
and lend to them
without expecting to get anything back.
Then your reward will be great. . .   LUKE 6:34,35

The shepherd who cares for his sheep

For this is what the Sovereign Lord says:
I myself will search for my sheep
and look after them.
As a shepherd looks after his scattered flock
when he is with them,
so will I look after my sheep.
I will rescue them from all the places
where they were scattered
on a day of clouds and darkness.
There they will lie down in good grazing land,
and there they will feed in a rich pasture
on the mountains of Israel.
I myself will tend my sheep
and make them lie down,
declares the Sovereign Lord.
I will search for the lost
and bring back the strays.
I will bind up the injured
and strengthen the weak.   EZEKIEL 34:11,12,14–16

I am the good shepherd;
I know my sheep and my sheep know me –
just as the Father knows me and I know
the Father –
and I lay down my life for the sheep.
I have other sheep
that are not of this sheep pen.
I must bring them also.
They too will listen to my voice,
and there shall be one flock
and one shepherd.   JOHN 10:14–16

Jesus the way to God

And a highway will be there;
it will be called the Way of Holiness.
The unclean will not journey on it . . .
wicked fools will not go about it. . .
But only the redeemed will walk there,
and the ransomed of the Lord will return.   ISAIAH 35:8,9,10

Thomas said to him,
'Lord, we don't know where you are going,
so how can we know the way?'
Jesus answered,
'I am the way and the truth and the life.
No-one comes to the Father except through me.
If you really knew me,
you would know my Father as well.
From now on, you do know him
and have seen him.'   JOHN 14:5–7

Enter through the narrow gate.
For wide is the gate and broad is the road
    that leads to destruction,
and many enter through it.
But small is the gate and narrow the road
    that leads to life,
and only a few find it.   MATTHEW 7:13,14

My feet have closely followed his steps;
I have kept to his way without turning aside.
I have not departed from the commands of his lips;
I have treasured the words of his mouth
    more than my daily bread.   JOB 23:11,12

The greatest commandment

One of the Pharisees, an expert in the law,
tested him with this question:
'Teacher, which is the greatest commandment
    in the Law?'
Jesus replied:
'Love the Lord your God with all your heart
and with all your soul and with all your mind.
This is the first and greatest commandment.'

MATTHEW 22:35–38

And God spoke all these words:
'I am the Lord your God,
who brought you out of Egypt,
out of the land of slavery.
You shall have no other gods before me.
You shall not make for yourself an idol
    in the form of anything in heaven above
or on the earth beneath
or in the waters below.
You shall not bow down to them or worship them;
for I, the Lord your God, am a jealous God. . .
You shall not misuse the name of the Lord your God,
for the Lord will not hold anyone guiltless
    who misuses his name.
Remember the Sabbath day by keeping it holy.
Six days you shall labour and do all your work,
but the seventh day is a Sabbath
    to the Lord your God.
Honour your father and your mother,
so that you may live long in the land
    the Lord your God is giving you.'

EXODUS 20:1–4,7–9,10,12

The second great commandment

The second most important commandment is this:
'Love your neighbour as yourself.'
There is no commandment
    greater than these.   MARK 12:31

A new commandment I give you:
Love one another.
As I have loved you,
so you must love one another.
All men will know that you are my disciples
if you love one another.   JOHN 13:34,35

Let no debt remain outstanding,
except the continuing debt to love one another,
for he who loves his fellow man
has fulfilled the law.
The commandments,
'Do not commit adultery,'
'Do not murder,'
'Do not steal,'
'Do not covet,'
and whatever other commandments there may be,
are summed up in this one rule:
'Love your neighbour as yourself.'
Love does no harm to its neighbour.
Therefore love is the fulfilment of the law.   ROMANS 13:8–10

All the Law and the Prophets
hang on these two commandments.   MATTHEW 22:40

The need to choose

We know that we are children of God,
and that the whole world is under the control
   of the evil one.
We know also that the Son of God has come
and has given us understanding,
so that we may know him who is true.
And we are in him who is true –
even in his Son Jesus Christ.
He is the true God and eternal life.
Dear children,
keep yourselves from idols.   1 JOHN 5:19–21

Joshua said to all the people. . .
'Now fear the Lord and serve him with all faithfulness.
Throw away the gods your forefathers worshipped
   beyond the River and in Egypt,
and serve the Lord.
But if serving the Lord seems undesirable to you,
then choose for yourselves this day
   whom you will serve. . .
But as for me and my household,
we will serve the Lord.'
And the people said to Joshua,
'We will serve the Lord our God and obey him.'
       JOSHUA 24:2,14,15,24

The Lord's message rang out from you
not only in Macedonia and Achaia –
your faith in God has become known everywhere.
Therefore we do not need to say anything about it,
for they themselves report
what kind of reception you gave us.
They tell how you turned to God from idols
to serve the living and true God.   1 THESSALONIANS 1:8,9

Choosing the true God

I tell you this, and insist on it in the Lord,
that you must no longer live as the Gentiles do,
in the futility of their thinking.
They are darkened in their understanding
and separated from the life of God
because of the ignorance that is in them
      due to the hardening of their hearts.
Having lost all sensitivity,
they have given themselves over to sensuality
so as to indulge in every kind of impurity,
with a continual lust for more.
You, however, did not come to know Christ that way.

EPHESIANS 4:17–20

For since the creation of the world
God's invisible qualities –
his eternal power and divine nature –
have been clearly seen,
being understood from what has been made,
so that men are without any excuse.
For although they knew God,
they neither glorified him as God
nor gave thanks to him,
but their thinking became futile
and their foolish hearts were darkened.

ROMANS 1:20,21

When the Counsellor comes,
he will convict the world of guilt
      in regard to sin
and righteousness
and judgement.

JOHN 16:8

The result of choosing other gods

They know nothing, they understand nothing;
their eyes are plastered over so they cannot see,
and their minds closed so they cannot understand.
No-one stops to think,
no-one has the knowledge or understanding to say,
'Half of it I used for fuel;
I even baked bread over its coals,
I roasted meat and I ate.
Shall I make a detestable thing from what is left?
Shall I bow down to a block of wood?'
He feeds on ashes, a deluded heart misleads him;
he cannot save himself, or say,
'Is not this thing in my right hand a lie?'   ISAIAH 44:18–20

Although they claimed to be wise,
they became fools
and exchanged the glory of the immortal God
for images made to look like mortal man
and birds and animals and reptiles.
Therefore God gave them over
     in the sinful desires of their hearts
to sexual impurity for the degrading of their bodies
     with one another.
They exchanged the truth of God for a lie,
and worshipped and served created things
rather than the Creator –
who is forever praised. Amen.   ROMANS 1:22–25

We receive as we have given

Do not be deceived:
God cannot be mocked.
A man reaps what he sows.
The one who sows to please his sinful nature,
from that nature will reap destruction;
the one who sows to please the Spirit,
from the Spirit will reap eternal life.
Let us not become weary in doing good,
for at the proper time we will reap a harvest
    if we do not give up.
Therefore, as we have opportunity,
let us do good to all people,
especially to those who belong
    to the family of believers.   GALATIANS 6:7–10

Be patient, then, brothers,
until the Lord's coming.
See how the farmer waits for the land to yield
    its valuable crop
and how patient he is for the autumn and spring rains.
You too, be patient and stand firm,
because the Lord's coming is near.   JAMES 5:7,8

Those who sow in tears
will reap with songs of joy.
He who goes out weeping,
carrying seed to sow,
will return with songs of joy,
carrying sheaves with him.   PSALM 126:5,6

God understands how we think and feel

The Lord said to Samuel,
'Do not consider his appearance or his height,
for I have rejected him.
The Lord does not look at the things man looks at.
Man looks at the outward appearance,
but the Lord looks at the heart.'   1 SAMUEL 16:7

The heart is deceitful above all things
        and beyond cure.
Who can understand it?
I the Lord search the heart and examine the mind,
to reward a man according to his conduct,
according to what his deeds deserve.   JEREMIAH 17:9,10

Nothing in all creation
        is hidden from God's sight.
Everything is uncovered and laid bare
        before the eyes of him
        to whom we must give account.   HEBREWS 4:13

O Lord, you have searched me and you know me.
You know when I sit and when I rise;
you perceive my thoughts from afar.
Before a word is on my tongue
you know it completely, O Lord.
Such knowledge is too wonderful for me,
too lofty for me to attain.   PSALM 139:1,2,4,6

We cannot hide from God

The Lord God called to the man,
'Where are you?'
He answered,
'I heard you in the garden,
and I was afraid because I was naked;
so I hid.'
And he said, 'Who told you that you were naked?
Have you eaten from the tree
that I commanded you not to eat from?'
The man said,
'The woman you put here with me –
she gave me some fruit from the tree,
and I ate it.'   GENESIS 3:9–12

Everyone who does evil hates the light,
and will not come into the light
for fear that his deeds will be exposed.
But whoever lives by the truth
        comes into the light,
so that it may be seen plainly
that what he has done
has been done through God.   JOHN 3:20,21

For you were once darkness,
but now you are light in the Lord.
Live as children of light.
Have nothing to do
        with the fruitless deeds of darkness,
but rather expose them.
For it is shameful even to mention
        what the disobedient do in secret.
But everything exposed by the light becomes visible,
for it is light that makes everything visible.
                          EPHESIANS 5:8,11–13,14

God knows us completely

Where can I go from your Spirit?
Where can I flee from your presence?
If I go up to the heavens, you are there;
if I make my bed in the depths, you are there.
If I rise on the wings of the dawn,
if I settle on the far side of the sea,
even there your hand will guide me,
your right hand will hold me fast.
If I say, 'Surely the darkness will hide me
and the light become night around me,'
even the darkness will not be dark to you;
the night will shine like the day,
for darkness is as light to you.   PSALM 139:7–12

Then the sailors said to each other,
'Come, let us cast lots to find out
who is responsible for this calamity.'
They cast lots and the lot fell on Jonah.
So they asked him, 'Tell us,
who is responsible for making all this trouble for us?
What do you do?
Where do you come from?
What is your country?
From what people are you?'
He answered, 'I am a Hebrew
and I worship the Lord, the God of heaven,
who made the sea and the land.'
This terrified them and they asked,
'What have you done?'
(They knew he was running away from the Lord,
because he had already told them so.)   JONAH 1:7–10

The foolishness of sinners

An oracle is within my heart
concerning the sinfulness of the wicked:
There is no fear of God before his eyes.
For in his own eyes he flatters himself
    too much to detect or hate his sin.
The words of his mouth are wicked and deceitful;
he has ceased to be wise and to do good.
Even on his bed he plots evil;
he commits himself to a sinful course
and does not reject what is wrong.   PSALM 36:1-4

For what hope has the godless
when he is cut off,
when God takes away his life?
Does God listen to his cry
when distress comes upon him?
Will he find delight in the Almighty?
Will he call upon God at all times?
I will teach you about the power of God;
the ways of the Almighty I will not conceal.
You have all seen this yourselves.
Why then this meaningless talk?   JOB 27:8-12

How great are your works, O Lord,
how profound your thoughts!
The senseless man does not know,
fools do not understand,
that though the wicked spring up like grass
and all evildoers flourish,
they will be for ever destroyed.
But you, O Lord, are exalted for ever.   PSALM 92:5-8

Persisting in sin

But our fathers refused to obey Moses.
Instead, they rejected him
and in their hearts turned back to Egypt.
But God turned away
and gave them over
  to the worship of the heavenly bodies. ACTS 7:39,42

In the desert
the whole community grumbled against Moses and Aaron.
The Israelites said to them,
'If only we had died by the Lord's hand in Egypt!
There we sat round pots of meat
and ate all the food we wanted. . . ' EXODUS 16:2,3

The people quarrelled with Moses and said,
'Give us water to drink.'
Moses replied,
'Why do you quarrel with me?
Why do you put the Lord to the test?' EXODUS 17:2,3

They wilfully put God to the test
by demanding the food they craved.
They spoke against God. . . PSALM 78:18,19

We should not test the Lord,
as some of them did –
and were killed by snakes.
And do not grumble, as some of them did –
and were killed by the destroying angel.
These things happened to them as examples
and were written down as warnings for us,
on whom the fulfilment of the ages has come.
  1 CORINTHIANS 10:9–11

The way of sinners

The wicked say to God, 'Leave us alone!
We have no desire to know your ways.
Who is the Almighty, that we should serve him?
What would we gain by praying to him?'
But their prosperity is not in their own hands,
so I stand aloof from the counsel of the wicked.

JOB 21:14–16

Blessed is the man
who does not walk in the counsel of the wicked
or stand in the way of sinners
or sit in the seat of mockers.
But his delight is in the law of the Lord,
and on his law he meditates day and night.
He is like a tree planted by streams of water,
which yields its fruit in season
and whose leaf does not wither.
Whatever he does prospers.

PSALM 1:1–3

This is the verdict:
Light has come into the world,
but men loved darkness instead of light
because their deeds were evil.
Everyone who does evil hates the light,
and will not come into the light
    for fear that his deeds will be exposed.
But whoever lives by the truth
    comes into the light,
so that it may be seen plainly
that what he has done
has been done through God.

JOHN 3:19–21

We must not blame anyone else

It is said, 'God stores up a man's punishment
for his sons.'
Let him repay the man himself,
so that he will know it!
Let his own eyes see his destruction;
let him drink of the wrath of the Almighty.   JOB 21:19,20

This is what the Lord Almighty,
the God of Israel, says:
'Just as I watched over them to uproot and tear down,
and to demolish, overthrow and bring disaster,
so I will watch over them to build and to plant,'
declares the Lord.
'In those days people will no longer say,
"The fathers have eaten sour grapes,
and the children's teeth are set on edge."
Instead everyone will die for his own sin;
whoever eats sour grapes,
his own teeth will be set on edge.'   JEREMIAH 31:23,28–30

Jesus' disciples asked him,
'Rabbi, who sinned, this man or his parents,
that he was born blind?'
'Neither this man nor his parents sinned,'
      said Jesus,
'but this happened so that the work of God
      might be displayed in his life.'   JOHN 9:2,3

February 3rd   Sin and responsibility

God forgives us when we admit our sins

If we claim to be without sin,
we deceive ourselves and the truth is not in us.
If we confess our sins,
he is faithful and just
and will forgive us our sins
and purify us from all unrighteousness.   1 JOHN 1:8,9

'Do not be afraid,' Samuel replied.
'You have done all this evil;
yet do not turn away from the Lord,
but serve the Lord with all your heart.
For the sake of his great name
the Lord will not reject his people,
because the Lord was pleased to make you his own.'

         1 SAMUEL 12:20,22

Blessed is he
whose transgressions are forgiven,
whose sins are covered.
Blessed is the man
whose sin the Lord does not count against him
and in whose spirit is no deceit.
When I kept silent, my bones wasted away
through my groaning all day long.
For day and night your hand was heavy upon me;
my strength was sapped as in the heat of summer.
Then I acknowledged my sin to you
and did not cover up my iniquity.
I said, 'I will confess
       my transgressions to the Lord' –
and you forgave the guilt of my sin.   PSALM 32:1–5

God wants our repentance

In those days John the Baptist came,
preaching in the Desert of Judea and saying,
'Repent, for the kingdom of heaven is near.'
People went out to him from Jerusalem and all Judea
        and the whole region of the Jordan.
Confessing their sins,
they were baptised by him in the Jordan River.

MATTHEW 3:1,2,5,6

Rend your heart and not your garments.
Return to the Lord your God,
for he is gracious and compassionate,
slow to anger and abounding in love,
and he relents from sending calamity.

JOEL 2:13

With what shall I come before the Lord
and bow down before the exalted God?
Shall I come before him with burnt offerings,
with calves a year old?
Will the Lord be pleased with thousands of rams,
with ten thousand rivers of oil?
Shall I offer my firstborn for my transgression,
the fruit of my body for the sin of my soul?
He has showed you, O man, what is good.
And what does the Lord require of you?
To act justly and to love mercy
and to walk humbly with your God.

MICAH 6:6–8

A complete change of life is needed

He who conceals his sins does not prosper,
but whoever confesses and renounces them finds mercy.
Blessed is the man who always fears the Lord,
but he who hardens his heart falls into trouble.

PROVERBS 28:13,14

'Even now,' declares the Lord,
'return to me with all your heart,
with fasting and weeping and mourning.'   JOEL 2:12

Return, O Israel, to the Lord your God.
Your sins have been your downfall!
Take words with you and return to the Lord.
Say to him:
'Forgive all our sins and receive us graciously,
that we may offer the fruit of our lips.
Assyria cannot save us;
we will not mount war-horses.
We will never again say "Our gods"
to what our own hands have made,
for in you the fatherless find compassion.'   HOSEA 14:1–3

Put off your old self

All the people . . . began to mutter,
'He has gone to be the guest of a "sinner".'
But Zacchaeus stood up and said to the Lord,
'Look, Lord!
Here and now I give half of my possessions to the poor,
and if I have cheated anybody out of anything,
I will pay back four times the amount.'
Jesus said to him,
'Today salvation has come to this house. . . '   LUKE 19:7–9

You were taught,
with regard to your former way of life,
to put off your old self,
which is being corrupted by its deceitful desires;
to be made new in the attitude of your minds;
and to put on the new self,
created to be like God
        in true righteousness and holiness.
He who has been stealing must steal no longer,
but must work,
doing something useful with his own hands,
that he may have something to share
        with those in need.
Do not let any unwholesome talk
come out of your mouths,
but only what is helpful for building others up
        according to their needs,
that it may benefit those who listen.
Be kind and compassionate to one another,
forgiving each other,
just as in Christ God forgave you.

                                    EPHESIANS 4:22–24,28,29,32

When we fall, God can lift us up again

David said to Nathan,
'I have sinned against the Lord.'
Nathan replied,
'The Lord has taken away your sin.
You are not going to die.
But because by doing this
you have made the enemies of the Lord
    show utter contempt,
the son born to you will die.'
After Nathan had gone home,
the Lord struck the child that Uriah's wife
    had borne to David,
and he became ill.
David pleaded with God for the child.
He fasted and went into his house
and spent the nights lying on the ground.
On the seventh day the child died. . .
Then David got up from the ground.
After he had washed,
put on lotions and changed his clothes,
he went into the house of the Lord and worshipped.

2 SAMUEL 12:13–16,18,20

I am laid low in the dust;
renew my life according to your word.
I recounted my ways and you answered me;
teach me your decrees.
Let me understand the teaching of your precepts;
then I will meditate on your wonders.
My soul is weary with sorrow;
strengthen me according to your word.
Keep me from deceitful ways;
be gracious to me through your law.

PSALM 119:25–29

Only God could save us

All of us also lived among them at one time,
gratifying the cravings of our sinful nature
and following its desires and thoughts.
Like the rest,
we were by nature objects of wrath.
But because of his great love for us,
God, who is rich in mercy,
made us alive with Christ
even when we were dead in transgressions –
it is by grace you have been saved.   EPHESIANS 2:3–5

I will praise you, O Lord.
Although you were angry with me,
your anger has turned away
and you have comforted me.
Surely God is my salavation;
I will trust and not be afraid.
The Lord, the Lord, is my strength and my song;
he has become my salvation.
With joy you will draw water
from the wells of salvation.   ISAIAH 12:1–3

All have sinned
and fall short of the glory of God,
and are justified freely by his grace
through the redemption
     that came by Christ Jesus.
God presented him
as a sacrifice of atonement,
through faith in his blood.   ROMANS 3:23–25

Confessing our sins to God

Blessed is he whose transgressions are forgiven,
whose sins are covered.
Blessed is the man
whose sin the Lord does not count against him
and in whose spirit is no deceit.
When I kept silent, my bones wasted away
through my groaning all day long.
For day and night your hand was heavy upon me;
my strength was sapped
as in the heat of summer.
Then I acknowledged my sin to you
and did not cover up my iniquity.
I said, 'I will confess my transgressions
        to the Lord' –
and you forgave the guilt of my sin.   PSALM 32:1–5

If we claim to be without sin,
we deceive ourselves and the truth is not in us.
If we confess our sins,
he is faithful and just
and will forgive us our sins
and purify us from all unrighteousness.
If we claim we have not sinned,
we make him out to be a liar
and his word has no place in our lives.
But if anybody does sin,
we have one who speaks to the Father
        in our defence –
Jesus Christ, the Righteous One.
He is the atoning sacrifice for our sins,
and not only for ours
but also for the sins of the whole world.   1 JOHN 1:8–10;2:1,2

God loves us despite everything

When Israel was a child, I loved him,
and out of Egypt I called my son.
But the more I called Israel,
the further they went from me.
They sacrificed to the Baals
and they burned incense to images.
It was I who taught Ephraim to walk,
taking them by the arms;
but they did not realise
     it was I who healed them.
I led them with cords of human kindness,
with ties of love;
I lifted the yoke from their neck
and bent down to feed them.   HOSEA 11:1–4

The son said to him
'Father, I have sinned against heaven
     and against you.
I am no longer worthy to be called your son.'
But the father said to his servants,
'Quick! Bring the best robe and put it on him.
Put a ring on his finger and sandals on his feet.
Bring the fatted calf and kill it.
Let's have a feast and celebrate.
For this son of mine was dead
     and is alive again;
he was lost and is found.'
So they began to celebrate.   LUKE 15:21–24

No matter how bad we think we are . . .

'Come now, let us reason together,'
says the Lord.
'Though your sins are like scarlet,
they shall be as white as snow;
though they are red as crimson,
they shall be like wool.'   ISAIAH 1:18

The Lord is compassionate and gracious,
slow to anger,
abounding in love.
He will not always accuse,
nor will he harbour his anger for ever;
he does not treat us as our sins deserve
or repay us according to our iniquities.
For as high as the heavens are above the earth,
so great is his love for those who fear him;
as far as the east is from the west,
so far has he removed our transgressions from us.
         PSALM 103:8–12

I write to you, dear children,
because your sins have been forgiven
     on account of his name.
I write to you, fathers,
because you have known him
     who is from the beginning.
I write to you, young men,
because you have overcome
     the evil one. . .
The world and its desires
pass away,
but the man who does the will of God
lives for ever.   1 JOHN 2:12,13,17

God accepts us through Jesus

He turned towards the woman
and said to Simon,
'Do you see this woman?
I came into your house.
You did not give me any water for my feet,
but she wet my feet with her tears
and wiped them with her hair.
You did not give me a kiss,
but this woman, from the time I entered,
has not stopped kissing my feet.
You did not put oil on my head,
but she has poured perfume on my feet.
Therefore, I tell you,
her many sins have been forgiven –
for she loved much.
But he who has been forgiven little
loves little.'
Then Jesus said to her,
'Your sins are forgiven.
Your faith has saved you; go in peace.'   LUKE 7:44–48, 50

Have mercy on me, O God,
according to your unfailing love;
according to your great compassion
blot out my transgressions.
Wash away all my iniquity
and cleanse me from my sin.
Cleanse me with hyssop, and I shall be clean;
wash me, and I shall be whiter than snow.
The sacrifices of God are a broken spirit;
a broken and contrite heart, O God,
you will not despise.   PSALM 51:1,2,7,17

Forgiveness for sins of the past

I have surely heard Ephraim's moaning:
'You disciplined me like an unruly calf,
and I have been disciplined.
Restore me, and I will return,
because you are the Lord my God.
After I strayed,
I repented;
after I came to understand,
I beat my breast.
I was ashamed and humiliated
because I bore the disgrace of my youth.'   JEREMIAH 31:18,19

Guide me in your truth and teach me,
for you are God my Saviour,
and my hope is in you all day long.
Remember, O Lord, your great mercy and love,
for they are from of old.
Remember not the sins of my youth.   PSALM 25:5–7

O Jerusalem, Jerusalem,
you who kill the prophets
and stone those sent to you,
how often I have longed
    to gather your children together,
as a hen gathers her chicks
    under her wings,
but you were not willing!   LUKE 13:34

God's promise to forgive

Then God said to Noah and to his sons with him:
'I now establish my covenant with you
and with your descendants after you
and with every living creature that was with you –
the birds, the livestock and all the wild animals. . .
Whenever I bring clouds over the earth
and the rainbow appears in the clouds,
I will remember my covenant between me and you
and all living creatures of every kind.
Never again will the waters become a flood
      to destroy all life.   GENESIS 9:8–10,14,15

'For a brief moment I abandoned you,
but with deep compassion I will bring you back.
In a surge of anger
I hid my face from you for a moment,
but with everlasting kindness
I will have compassion on you.'
says the Lord your Redeemer.
'To me this is like the days of Noah,
when I swore that the waters of Noah
would never again cover the earth.
So now I have sworn not to be angry with you,
never to rebuke you again.
Though the mountains be shaken
and the hills be removed,
yet my unfailing love for you will not be shaken
nor my covenant of peace be removed,'
says the Lord, who has compassion on you.   ISAIAH 54:7–10

Sing to the Lord, you saints of his;
praise his holy name.
For his anger lasts only a moment,
but his favour lasts a lifetime.   PSALM 30:4,5

God can forgive us through Christ

Since we have a great high priest
who has gone through the heavens,
Jesus the Son of God,
let us hold firmly to the faith we profess.
For we do not have a high priest
who is unable to sympathise with our weaknesses,
but we have one
who has been tempted in every way,
just as we are – yet was without sin.
Let us then approach the throne of grace
    with confidence,
so that we may receive mercy
and find grace to help us
    in our time of need.   HEBREWS 4:14–16

Therefore, there is now no condemnation
    for those who are in Christ Jesus,
because through Christ Jesus
the law of the Spirit of life set me free
    from the law of sin and death.
For what the law was powerless to do
in that it was weakened by the sinful nature,
God did by sending his own Son
    in the likeness of sinful man
to be a sin offering.
And so he condemned sin in sinful man.   ROMANS 8:1–3

We must forgive others

Then Peter came to Jesus and asked,
'Lord, how many times shall I forgive my brother
    when he sins against me?
Up to seven times?'
Jesus answered, 'I tell you, not seven times,
but seventy-seven times.'   MATTHEW 18:21,22

The master called the servant in.
'You wicked servant,' he said,
'I cancelled all that debt of yours
because you begged me to.
Shouldn't you have had mercy on your fellow servant
just as I had on you?'
In anger his master turned him over to the jailers
until he should pay back all he owed.
This is how my heavenly Father
will treat each of you
unless you forgive your brother from your heart.
         MATTHEW 18:32–35

Be kind and compassionate to one another,
forgiving each other,
just as in Christ God forgave you.   EPHESIANS 4:32

Our Father in heaven. . .
Forgive us our debts,
as we also have forgiven
    our debtors.   MATTHEW 6:9,12

Assurance that we belong to God

Everyone who loves
has been born of God and knows God.
Whoever does not love does not know God,
because God is love.
This is how God showed his love among us:
He sent his one and only Son into the world
that we might live through him.
This is love:
not that we loved God, but that he loved us
and sent his Son
as an atoning sacrifice for our sins.   1 JOHN 4:7–10

For God so loved the world
that he gave his one and only Son,
that whoever believes in him shall not perish
but have eternal life.
For God did not send his Son into the world
to condemn the world,
but to save the world through him.   JOHN 3:16–17

For I am convinced
that neither death nor life,
neither angels nor demons,
neither the present nor the future,
nor any powers,
neither height nor depth,
nor anything else in all creation,
will be able to separate us from the love of God
that is in Christ Jesus our Lord.   ROMANS 8:38,39

Being confident that God accepts us

This then is how we know
    that we belong to the truth,
and how we set our hearts at rest in his presence
    whenever our hearts condemn us.
For God is greater than our hearts,
and he knows everything.
And this is how we know that he lives in us:
We know it by the Spirit he gave us.   1 JOHN 3:19,20,24

He who dwells in the shelter of the Most High
will rest in the shadow of the Almighty.
I will say of the Lord,
'He is my refuge and my fortress,
 my God, in whom I trust.'
'Because he loves me,' says the Lord,
'I will rescue him;
I will protect him, for he acknowledges my name.
He will call upon me, and I will answer him;
I will be with him in trouble,
I will deliver him and honour him.'   PSALM 91:1,2,14,15

My sheep listen to my voice;
I know them, and they follow me.
I give them eternal life,
and they shall never perish;
no-one can snatch them out of my hand.
My Father, who has given them to me,
    is greater than all;
no-one can snatch them
    out of my Father's hand.
I and the Father are one.   JOHN 10:27–30

Being sure that we have eternal life

I write these things
to you who believe
   in the name of the Son of God
so that you may know that you have eternal life.
This is the assurance we have in approaching God:
that if we ask anything according to his will,
he hears us.
And if we know that he hears us –
   whatever we ask –
we know that we have what we asked of him.

1 JOHN 5:13–15

Jesus said, 'Do not let your hearts be troubled.
Trust in God; trust also in me.
In my Father's house are many rooms;
if it were not so, I would have told you.
I am going there to prepare a place for you.
And if I go and prepare a place for you,
I will come back and take you to be with me
that you also may be where I am.'

JOHN 14:1–3

But the other criminal rebuked him.
'. . . We are punished justly,
for we are getting what our deeds deserve.
But this man has done nothing wrong.'
Then he said,
'Jesus, remember me when you come
   into your kingdom.'
Jesus answered him,
'I tell you the truth,
today you will be with me in paradise.'

LUKE 23:40,41–43

Hope in spite of death

'Lord,' Martha said to Jesus
'if you had been here,
  my brother would not have died.
But I know that even now
      God will give you whatever you ask.'
Jesus said to her, 'Your brother will rise again.'
Martha answered, 'I know he will rise again
in the resurrection at the last day.'
Jesus said to her,
'I am the resurrection and the life.
He who believes in me will live,
  even though he dies;
and whoever lives and believes in me
will never die.
Do you believe this?'
'Yes, Lord,' she told him,
'I believe that you are the Christ,
  the Son of God,
who was to come into the world.'   JOHN 11:21–27

Brothers,
we do not want you to be ignorant,
      about those who fall asleep,
or to grieve like the rest of men,
who have no hope.
We believe that Jesus died and rose again
and so we believe
      that God will bring with Jesus
those who have fallen asleep in him.
And so we will be with the Lord for ever.
Therefore encourage each other with these words.
                              1 THESSALONIANS 4:13,14,18

February 21st   The troubled mind

When life is too hard

I cry aloud to the Lord;
I lift up my voice to the Lord for mercy.
I pour out my complaint before him;
before him I tell my trouble.
When my spirit grows faint within me,
it is you who know my way.   PSALM 142:1–3

Elijah went a day's journey into the desert.
He came to a broom tree, sat down under it
and prayed that he might die.
'I have had enough, Lord,' he said.
'Take my life; I am no better than
      my ancestors.'
Then he lay down under the tree
and fell asleep.
All at once an angel touched him and said . . .
'Get up and eat,
for the journey is too much for you.'
So he got up and ate and drank.
Strengthened by that food,
he travelled for forty days and forty nights
until he reached Horeb, the mountain of God.
There he went into a cave and spent the night.
                              1 KINGS 19:4,5,7,8,9

O God, you are my God, earnestly I seek you;
my soul thirsts for you, my body longs for you,
      in a dry and weary land where there is no water.
I have seen you in the sanctuary
and beheld your power and your glory.
Because your love is better than life,
my lips will glorify you.
I will praise you as long as I live,
and in your name I will lift up my hands.

                              PSALM 63:1–5

Facing opposition

And the word of the Lord came to him:
'What are you doing here, Elijah?'
He replied,
'I have been very zealous
        for the Lord God Almighty.
The Israelites have rejected your covenant,
broken down your altars,
and put your prophets to death with the sword.
I am the only one left,
and now they are trying to kill me too.'
The Lord said, 'Go out
and stand on the mountain in the presence
        of the Lord,
for the Lord is about to pass by.'
Then a great and powerful wind
tore the mountains apart
and shattered the rocks before the Lord,
but the Lord was not in the wind.
After the wind there was an earthquake,
but the Lord was not in the earthquake.
After the earthquake came a fire,
but the Lord was not in the fire.
And after the fire came a gentle whisper.
When Elijah heard it,
he pulled his cloak over his face
and went out and stood at the mouth of the cave.
Then a voice said to him,
'What are you doing here, Elijah?'   1 KINGS 19:9–13

The experience of Jesus

My God, my God, why have you forsaken me?
Why are you so far from saving me,
so far from the words of my groaning?
O my God, I cry out by day,
    but you do not answer,
by night, and am not silent.   PSALM 22:1,2

At the sixth hour
darkness came over the whole land
until the ninth hour.
And at the ninth hour Jesus cried out
    in a loud voice,
'*Eloi, Eloi, lama sabachthani?*' –
which means,
'My God, my God, why have you forsaken me?'   MARK 15:33,34

Yet it was the Lord's will
to crush him and cause him to suffer,
and though the Lord makes his life
    a guilt offering,
he will see his offspring and prolong his days,
and the will of the Lord
will prosper in his hand.
After the suffering of his soul,
he will see the light of life
and be satisfied;
by his knowledge
my righteous servant will justify many,
and he will bear their inquities.
Therefore I will give him
a portion among the great,
and he will divide the spoils with the strong,
because he poured out his life unto death,
and was numbered with the transgressors.   ISAIAH 53:10–12

Far from home

By the rivers of Babylon we sat
and wept when we remembered Zion.
There on the poplars
we hung our harps,
for there our captors asked us for songs,
our tormentors demanded songs of joy;
they said, 'Sing us one of the songs of Zion!'
How can we sing the songs of the Lord
while in a foreign land?   PSALM 137:1–4

David longed for water and said,
'Oh, that someone would get me a drink
     of water
from the well near the gate of Bethlehem!'
So the three mighty men
broke through the Philistine lines,
drew water from the well
near the gate of Bethlehem
and carried it back to David.
But he refused to drink it;
instead, he poured it out before the Lord.   2 SAMUEL 23:15,16

For here we do not have an enduring city,
but we are looking for the city
that is to come.   HEBREWS 13:14

Praise the Lord.
How good it is to sing praises to our God,
how pleasant and fitting to praise him!
The Lord builds up Jerusalem;
he gathers the exiles of Israel.
He heals the broken-hearted
and binds up their wounds.   PSALM 147:1–3

Doubt and questioning

Why do the wicked live on,
growing old and increasing in power?
They see their children established around them,
their offspring before their eyes.
Their homes are safe and free from fear;
the rod of God is not upon them.
They spend their years in prosperity
and go down to the grave in peace.   JOB 21:7–9,13

When the angel of the Lord appeared to Gideon,
he said,
'The Lord is with you, mighty warrior.'
'But sir,' Gideon replied,
'if the Lord is with us,
    why has all this happened us us?
Where are all his wonders
that our fathers told us about when they said,
"Did not the Lord bring us up out of Egypt?"
But now the Lord has abandoned us
and put us into the hand of Midian.'
The Lord turned to him and said,
'Go in the strength you have
and save Israel out of Midian's hand.
Am I not sending you?'   JUDGES 6:12–14

Lord, I have heard of your fame;
I stand in awe of your deeds, O Lord.
Renew them in our day,
in our time make them known;
in wrath remember mercy.   HABAKKUK 3:2

Questioning God

Even today my complaint is bitter;
his hand is heavy in spite of my groaning.
If only I knew where to find him;
if only I could go to his dwelling!
But if I go to the east, he is not there;
if I go to the west, I do not find him.
When he is at work in the north,
I do not see him;
when he turns to the south,
I catch no glimpse of him.   JOB 23:2,3,8,9

'Do not let your hearts be troubled.
Trust in God; trust also in me.
You know the way
        to the place where I am going.'
Thomas said to him,
'Lord, we don't know where you are going,
so how can we know the way?'
Jesus answered,
'I am the way and the truth and the life.
No-one comes to the Father except through me.
If you really knew me,
you would know my Father as well.
From now on, you do know him
and have seen him.'   JOHN 14:1,4–7

More than conquerors

As servants of God
we commend ourselves in every way. . .
through glory and dishonour,
bad report and good report;
genuine, yet regarded as imposters;
known, yet regarded as unknown;
dying, and yet we live on;
beaten, and yet not killed;
sorrowful, yet always rejoicing;
poor, yet making many rich;
having nothing, and yet possessing everything.

2 CORINTHIANS 6:4,8–10

Who shall separate us
from the love of Christ?
Shall trouble or hardship
or persecution or famine
or nakedness or danger or sword?
As it is written:
'For your sake we face death
    all day long;
we are considered as sheep
    to be slaughtered.'
No, in all these things
we are more than conquerors
through him who loved us.

ROMANS 8:35–37

Praise through pain

Consider it pure joy, my brothers,
whenever you face trials of many kinds,
because you know
    that the testing of your faith
develops perseverance.
Perseverance must finish its work
so that you may be mature and complete,
not lacking anything.
                         JAMES 1:2–4

Though the fig-tree does not bud
and there are no grapes on the vines,
though the olive crop fails
and the fields produce no food,
though there are no sheep in the pen
and no cattle in the stalls,
yet I will rejoice in the Lord,
I will be joyful in God my Saviour.
              HABAKKUK 3:17,18

Even though I walk through the valley of
    the shadow of death,
I will fear no evil,
for you are with me;
your rod and staff, they comfort me.
You prepare a table before me
in the presence of my enemies.
You anoint my head with oil;
my cup overflows.
Surely goodness and love will follow me
all the days of my life,
and I will dwell in the house of the Lord
for ever.
                    PSALM 23:4–6

The healing power of the Lord

When she heard about Jesus,
she came up behind him in the crowd
and touched his cloak,
because she thought,
'If I just touch his clothes,
I will be healed.'
Immediately her bleeding stopped
and she felt in her body
that she was freed from her suffering.
The woman, knowing what had happened to her,
came and fell at his feet
and, trembling with fear, told him
the whole truth.
He said to her,
'Daughter, your faith has healed you.
Go in peace and be freed from your suffering.'

MARK 5:27–29,33,34

O Lord, do not rebuke me in your anger
or discipline me in your wrath.
Be merciful to me, Lord, for I am faint;
O Lord, heal me, for my bones are in agony.
My soul is in anguish.
How long, O Lord, how long?
I am worn out with groaning;
all night long I flood my bed with weeping
and drench my couch with tears.
My eyes grow weak with sorrow;
they fail because of all my foes.
Away from me, all you who do evil,
for the Lord has heard my weeping.
The Lord has heard my cry for mercy;
the Lord accepts my prayer.

PSALM 6:1–3, 6–9

God brings hope again

I have been deprived of peace;
I have forgotten what prosperity is.
So I say, 'My splendour is gone
and all that I had hoped from the Lord.'
I remember my affliction and my wandering,
the bitterness and the gall.
I well remember them,
and my soul is downcast within me.
Yet this I call to mind
and therefore I have hope:
Because of the Lord's great love
we are not consumed,
for his compassions never fail.
They are new every morning;
great is your faithfulness.
I say to myself, 'The Lord is my portion;
therefore I will wait for him.'   LAMENTATIONS 3:17–24

I will exalt you, O Lord,
for you lifted me out of the depths
and did not let my enemies gloat over me.
O Lord my God, I called to you for help
and you healed me.
O Lord, you brought me up from the grave;
you spared me from going down into the pit.
Sing to the Lord, you saints of his;
praise his holy name.
For his anger lasts only a moment,
but his favour lasts a lifetime;
weeping may remain for a night,
but rejoicing comes in the morning.   PSALM 30:1–5

The healing church

Calling the Twelve to him,
he sent them out two by two
and gave them authority over evil spirits.
These were his instructions:
'Take nothing for the journey
except a staff –
no bread, no bag,
no money in your belts.'
They went out
and preached that people should repent.
They drove out many demons
and anointed many sick people with oil
and healed them.   MARK 6:7,8,12,13

Is any one of you sick?
He should call the elders of the church
to pray over him
and anoint him with oil
in the name of the Lord.
And the prayer offered in faith
will make the sick person well;
the Lord will raise him up.
If he has sinned, he will be forgiven.
Therefore confess your sins to each other
and pray for each other
so that you may be healed.
The prayer of a righteous man
is powerful and effective.   JAMES 5:14–16

The Lord who delivers

Heal me, O Lord,
and I shall be healed;
save me and I shall be saved,
for you are the one I praise.   JEREMIAH 17:14

The Lord sent venomous snakes among them;
they bit the people
and many Israelites died.
The people came to Moses and said,
'We sinned
when we spoke against the Lord
and against you.
Pray that the Lord will take the snakes
          away from us.'
So Moses prayed for the people.
The Lord said to Moses,
'Make a snake and put it up on a pole;
anyone who is bitten can look at it
and live.'   NUMBERS 21:6–9

Just as Moses lifted up the snake
in the desert,
so the Son of Man must be lifted up,
that everyone who believes
may have eternal life in him.
For God so loved the world
that he gave his one and only Son,
that whoever believes in him
shall not perish but have eternal life.   JOHN 3:14–16

The healing Lord

'Surely the day is coming;
it will burn like a furnace.
All the arrogant and every evildoer
    will be stubble,
and that day that is coming
will set them on fire,'
says the Lord Almighty.
'Not a root or a branch will be left to them.
But for you who revere my name,
the sun of righteousness will rise
with healing in its wings.
And you will go out and leap like calves
released from the stall.'   MALACHI 4:1,2

Praise the Lord, O my soul;
all my inmost being, praise his holy name.
Praise the Lord, O my soul,
and forget not all his benefits.
He forgives all my sins
and heals all my diseases;
he redeems my life from the pit
and crowns me with love and compassion.
He satisfies my desires with good things,
so that my youth is renewed like the eagle's.   PSALM 103:1–5

Praying for forgiveness

We have sinned, we have done wrong.
O Lord, in keeping with all your righteous acts,
turn away your anger and your wrath from Jerusalem,
your city, your holy hill. . .
Now, our God,
hear the prayers and petitions of your servant.
For your sake, O Lord, look with favour
on your desolate sanctuary.
Give ear, O God, and hear;
open your eyes and see the desolation of the city
        that bears your name.
We do not make requests of you
        because we are righteous,
but because of your great mercy.
O Lord, listen! O Lord, forgive!
O Lord, hear and act!
For your sake, O my God, do not delay,
because your city and your people bear your Name.

DANIEL 9:15,16,17–19

I revealed myself to those who did not ask for me;
I was found by those who did not seek me.
To a nation that did not call on my name,
I said, 'Here am I, here am I.'
All day long I have held out my hands
to an obstinate people,
who walk in ways not good,
pursuing their own imaginations.   ISAIAH 65:1,2

Praying to a loving Father

Your Father knows what you need
before you ask him.
This is how you should pray:
'Our Father in heaven,
hallowed be your name,
your kingdom come,
your will be done
on earth as it is in heaven.
Give us today our daily bread.
Forgive us our debts,
as we also have forgiven our debtors.
And lead us not into temptation,
but deliver us from the evil one.'
For if you forgive men
when they sin against you,
your heavenly Father
will also forgive you.   MATTHEW 6:8–14

The Lord is compassionate and gracious,
slow to anger, abounding in love.
He will not always accuse,
nor will he harbour his anger for ever;
he does not treat us as our sins deserve
or repay us according to our iniquities.
For as high as the heavens are above the earth,
so great is his love for those who fear him;
as far as the east is from the west,
so far has he removed our transgressions from us.
As a father has compassion on his children,
so the Lord has compassion on those who fear him.
                                        PSALM 103:8–13

Praying as a son

Going a little farther,
Jesus fell to the ground and prayed
that if possible the hour might pass from him.
'*Abba*, Father,' he said,
'everything is possible for you.
Take this cup from me.
Yet not what I will, but what you will.'   MARK 14:35,36

You did not receive a spirit
that makes you a slave again to fear,
but you received the Spirit of sonship.
And by him we cry, '*Abba*, Father.'
The Spirit himself testifies with our spirit
that we are God's children.
Now if we are children, then we are heirs –
heirs of God and co-heirs with Christ,
if indeed we share in his sufferings
in order that we may also share in his glory.

ROMANS 8:15–17

Because you are sons,
God sent the Spirit of his Son into our hearts,
the Spirit who calls out, '*Abba*, Father.'
So you are no longer a slave, but a son;
and since you are a son,
God has made you also an heir.   GALATIANS 4:6,7

Praying persistently

Suppose one of you has a friend,
and he goes to him at midnight and says,
'Friend, lend me three loaves of bread,
because a friend of mine on a journey
has come to me,
and I have nothing to set before him.'
Then the one inside answers,
'Don't bother me.
The door is already locked,
and my children are with me in bed.
I can't get up and give you anything.'
I tell you,
though he will not get up and give him the bread
because he is his friend,
yet because of the man's persistence
he will get up
and give him as much as he needs.   LUKE 11:5–8

When Bartimaeus heard
that it was Jesus of Nazareth,
he began to shout,
'Jesus, Son of David, have mercy on me!'
Many rebuked him and told him to be quiet,
but he shouted all the more,
'Son of David, have mercy on me!'
Jesus stopped and said,
'Call him.'   MARK 10:47–49

Praying is an opportunity

Seek the Lord while he may be found;
call on him while he is near.
Let the wicked forsake his way
and the evil man his thoughts.
Let him turn to the Lord,
and he will have mercy on him,
and to our God, for he will freely pardon.   ISAIAH 55:6,7

'I know the plans I have for you,'
declares the Lord,
'plans to prosper you and not to harm you,
plans to give you hope and a future.
Then you will call upon me
and come and pray to me,
and I will listen to you.
You will seek me and find me
when you seek me with all your heart.'   JEREMIAH 29:11–13

I say to you:
Ask and it will be given to you;
seek and you will find;
knock and the door will be opened to you.
For everyone who asks receives;
he who seeks finds;
and to him who knocks,
the door will be opened.   LUKE 11:9,10

Praying in faith

I tell you the truth,
anyone who has faith in me
will do what I have been doing.
He will do even greater things than these,
because I am going to the Father.
And I will do whatever you ask in my name,
so that the Son may bring glory to the Father.
You may ask me for anything in my name,
and I will do it.

JOHN 14:12–14

'In the whole land,' declares the Lord,
'two-thirds will be struck down and perish;
yet one-third will be left in it.
This third I will bring into the fire;
I will refine them like silver and test them like gold.
They will call on my name and I will answer them;
I will say, "They are my people,"
and they will say, "The Lord is our God." '

ZECHARIAH 13:8,9

Now is your time of grief,
but I will see you again and you will rejoice,
and no-one will take away your joy.
In that day you will no longer ask me anything.
I tell you the truth,
my Father will give you whatever you ask in my name.
Until now you have not asked for anything in my name.
Ask and you will receive,
and your joy will be complete.

JOHN 16:22–24

The attractiveness of the world

Do not love the world
or anything in the world.
If anyone loves the world,
the love of the Father is not in him.
For everything in the world –
the cravings of sinful man,
the lust of his eyes
and the boasting of what he has and does –
comes not from the Father
but from the world.
The world and its desires pass away,
but the man who does the will of God
      lives for ever.   1 JOHN 2:15–17

The devil led him up to a high place
and showed him in an instant
      all the kingdoms of the world.
And he said to him,
'I will give you all their authority and splendour,
for it has been given to me,
and I can give it to anyone I want to.
So if you worship me, it will all be yours.'
Jesus answered,
'It is written:
"Worship the Lord your God
and serve him only." '   LUKE 4:5–8

The element of doubt

Now the serpent was more crafty
than any of the wild animals
    the Lord God had made.
He said to the woman,
'Did God really say,
"You must not eat from any tree in the garden"?'
The woman said to the serpent,
'We may eat fruit from the trees in the garden,
but God did say,
"You must not eat fruit from the tree
that is in the middle of the garden,
and you must not touch it,
or you will die." '
'You will not surely die,'
the serpent said to the woman.
'For God knows that when you eat of it
your eyes will be opened,
and you will be like God,
knowing good and evil.'
When the woman saw that the fruit of the tree
was good for food and pleasing to the eye,
and also desirable for gaining wisdom,
she took some and ate it.
She also gave some to her husband, who was with her,
and he ate it.   GENESIS 3:1–6

When the people saw that Moses was so long
in coming down from the mountain,
they gathered around Aaron and said,
'Come, make us gods who will go before us.
As for this fellow Moses
who brought us up out of Egypt,
we don't know what has happened to him.'   EXODUS 32:1

Know your enemy!

Finally, be strong in the Lord
and in his mighty power.
Put on the full armour of God
so that you can take your stand
against the devil's schemes.
For our struggle is not against flesh and blood,
but against the rulers,
against the authorities,
against the powers of this dark world
and against the spiritual forces of evil
in the heavenly realms.
Therefore put on the full armour of God,
so that when the day of evil comes,
you may be able to stand your ground,
and after you have done everything,
to stand.   EPHESIANS 6:10–13

So, if you think you are standing firm,
be careful that you don't fall!
No temptation has seized you
except what is common to man.
And God is faithful;
he will not let you be tempted beyond
     what you can bear.
But when you are tempted,
he will also provide a way out
so that you can stand up under it.   1 CORINTHIANS 10:12,13

Know your weakness

'Simon, Simon,
Satan has asked to sift you as wheat.
But I have prayed for you, Simon,
that your faith may not fail.
And when you have turned back,
strengthen your brothers.'
But he replied, 'Lord,
I am ready to go with you to prison and to death.'
Jesus answered, 'I tell you, Peter,
before the cock crows today,
you will deny three times that you know me.'   LUKE 22:31–34

Be self-controlled and alert.
Your enemy the devil
prowls around like a roaring lion
looking for someone to devour.
Resist him, standing firm in the faith,
because you know that your brothers
     throughout the world
are undergoing the same kind of sufferings.
And the God of all grace,
who called you to his eternal glory in Christ,
after you have suffered a little while,
will himself restore you and make you strong,
     firm and steadfast.   1 PETER 5:8–10

Recognising our inadequacy

Do you think Scripture says without reason
that the spirit he caused to live in us
    tends towards envy,
but he gives us more grace?
That is why Scripture says:
'God opposes the proud
but gives grace to the humble.'
Submit yourselves, then, to God.
Resist the devil, and he will flee from you.
Come near to God
and he will come near to you. . .   JAMES 4:5–8

Have mercy on me, O God,
according to your unfailing love;
according to your great compassion
blot out my transgressions.
Wash away all my iniquity
and cleanse me from my sin.
For I know my transgressions,
and my sin is always before me.
Against you, you only, have I sinned
and done what is evil in your sight,
so that you are proved right when you speak
and justified when you judge.
Surely I have been a sinner from birth,
sinful from the time my mother conceived me.
You do not delight in sacrifice, or I would bring it;
you do not take pleasure in burnt offerings.
The sacrifices of God are a broken spirit;
a broken and contrite heart,
O God, you will not despise.   PSALM 51:1–5,16,17

A prisoner of the law of sin

After a little while,
those standing near said to Peter,
'Surely you are one of them,
for you are a Galilean.'
He began to call down curses on himself,
and he swore to them,
'I don't know this man
you're talking about.'
Immediately the cock crowed the second time.
Then Peter remembered the word Jesus had spoken to him:
'Before the rooster crows twice
you will disown me three times.'
And he broke down and wept.   MARK 14:70–72

So I find this law at work:
When I want to do good,
evil is right there with me.
For in my inner being I delight in God's law;
but I see another law at work
     in the members of my body,
waging war against the law of my mind
and making me a prisoner of the law of sin
     at work within my members.
What a wretched man I am!
Who will rescue me from this body of death?
Thanks be to God –
through Jesus Christ our Lord!   ROMANS 7:21–25

March 17th   Temptation and testing

God can rescue us

If God condemned the cities of Sodom and Gomorrah
by burning them to ashes,
and made them an example of what is going to happen
    to the ungodly;
and if he rescued Lot, a righteous man,
who was distressed by the filthy lives of lawless men
(for that righteous man,
living among them day after day,
was tormented in his righteous soul
by the lawless deeds he saw and heard) –
if this is so,
then the Lord knows how to rescue godly men from trials
and to hold the unrighteous for the day of judgement,
while continuing their punishment.   2 PETER 2:6–9

When Lot hesitated,
the men grasped his hand
and the hands of his wife and of his two daughters
and led them safely out of the city,
for the Lord was merciful to them.
As soon as they had brought them out,
one of them said,
'Flee for your lives!
Don't look back, and don't stop anywhere in the plain!
Flee to the mountains or you will be swept away!'
By the time Lot reached Zoar,
the sun had risen over the land.
Then the Lord rained down burning sulphur
    on Sodom and Gomorrah –
from the Lord out of the heavens.
Thus he overthrew those cities and the entire plain,
including all those living in the cities –
and also the vegetation in the land.   GENESIS 19:16,17,23–25

Be glad about testing

Then Abraham reached out his hand
and took the knife to slay his son.
But the angel of the Lord
called out to him from heaven,
'Abraham! Abraham!'
'Here I am,' he replied.
'Do not lay a hand on the boy,' he said.
'Do not do anything to him.
Now I know that you fear God,
because you have not withheld from me your son,
    your only son.'
The angel of the Lord called to Abraham from heaven
    a second time and said,
'I swear by myself, declares the Lord,
that because you have done this
and have not withheld your son, your only son,
I will surely bless you. . . '   GENESIS 22:10–12,15,16,17

In this you greatly rejoice,
though now for a little while
you may have had to suffer grief
in all kinds of trials.
These have come so that your faith –
of greater worth than gold,
which perishes even though refined by fire –
may be proved genuine
and may result in praise, glory and honour
when Jesus Christ is revealed.   1 PETER 1:6,7

Happy are those who are persecuted!

Dear friends,
do not be surprised
at the painful trial you are suffering,
as though something strange were happening to you.
But rejoice that you participate
        in the sufferings of Christ,
so that you may be overjoyed when his glory is revealed.
If you are insulted because of the name of Christ,
you are blessed,
for the Spirit of glory and of God rests on you.
If you suffer as a Christian, do not be ashamed,
but praise God that you bear that name.   1 PETER 4:12–14,16

I hear many whispering, 'Terror on every side!
Report him! Let's report him!'
All my friends are waiting for me to slip, saying,
'Perhaps he will be deceived;
then we will prevail over him
and take our revenge on him.'
O Lord Almighty, you who examine the righteous
and probe the heart and mind,
let me see your vengeance upon them,
for to you I have committed my cause.   JEREMIAH 20:10,12

Blessed are those who are persecuted
        because of righteousness,
for theirs is the kingdom of heaven.
Blessed are you when people insult you, persecute you
and falsely say all kinds of evil against you
        because of me.
Rejoice and be glad,
because great is your reward in heaven,
for in the same way they persecuted the prophets
        who were before you.   MATTHEW 5:10–12

The coming of the King

Rejoice greatly; O Daughter of Zion!
Shout, daughter of Jerusalem!
See, your king comes to you,
righteous and having salvation,
gentle and riding on a donkey,
on a colt, the foal of a donkey.   ZECHARIAH 9:9

When the disciples brought the colt to Jesus
and threw their cloaks over it,
he sat on it.
Many people spread their cloaks on the road,
while others spread branches they had cut
     in the fields.
Those who went ahead and those who followed shouted,
'Hosanna!
Blessed is he who comes in the name of the Lord!
Blessed is the coming kingdom of our father David!
Hosanna in the highest!'   MARK 11:7–10

Blessed is he
who comes in the name of the Lord.
From the house of the Lord we bless you.
The Lord is God,
and he has made his light shine upon us.
With boughs in hand, join in the festal procession
up to the horns of the altar.   PSALM 118:26,27

Clearing out the Temple of God

Hezekiah said, 'Listen to me, Levites!
Consecrate yourselves now
and consecrate the temple of the Lord,
    the God of your fathers.
Remove all defilement from the sanctuary.
Our fathers were unfaithful;
they did evil in the eyes of the Lord our God
    and forsook him.'
The priests went into the sanctuary of the Lord
    to purify it.
They brought out to the courtyard of the Lord's temple
everything unclean that they found
    in the temple of the Lord.   2 CHRONICLES 29:5,6,16

'See, I will send my messenger,
who will prepare the way before me.
Then suddenly the Lord you are seeking
    will come to his temple;
the messenger of the covenant, whom you desire,
    will come,'
says the Lord Almighty.
But who can endure the day of his coming?
Who can stand when he appears?   MALACHI 3:1,2

Jesus entered the temple area
and drove out all who were buying and selling there.
He overturned the tables of the money-changers
and the benches of those selling doves.
'It is written,' he said to them,
' "My house will be called a house of prayer,"
but you are making it a "den of robbers".'
The blind and the lame came to him at the temple,
and he healed them.   MATTHEW 21:12–14

The new agreement God has made with us

'The time is coming,' declares the Lord,
'when I will make a new covenant
with the house of Israel and with the house of Judah.
This is the covenant
that I will make with the house of Israel
        after that time,' declares the Lord.
'I will put my law in their minds
and write it on their hearts.
I will be their God, and they will be my people.
No longer will a man teach his neighbour,
or a man his brother, saying,
"Know the Lord,"
because they will all know me,
from the least of them to the greatest,'
        declares the Lord.
'For I will forgive their wickedness
and will remember their sins no more.'

JEREMIAH 31:31,33,34

While they were eating,
Jesus took bread, gave thanks and broke it,
and gave it to his disciples, saying,
'Take and eat; this is my body.'
Then he took the cup, gave thanks
and offered it to them, saying,
'Drink from it, all of you.
This is my blood of the covenant,
which is poured out for many
for the forgiveness of sins.'   MATTHEW 26:26–28

Christ is the mediator of a new covenant,
that those who are called
may receive the promised eternal inheritance –
now that he has died as a ransom
to set them free from the sins committed
        under the first covenant.   HEBREWS 9:15

Jesus: priest and victim

When any of you brings an offering to the Lord,
bring as your offering
an animal from either the herd or the flock.
If the offering is a burnt offering from the herd,
he is to offer a male without defect.
He must present it
    at the entrance to the Tent of Meeting
so that it will be acceptable to the Lord.
He is to lay his hand on the head of the burnt offering,
and it will be accepted on his behalf
    to make atonement for him.   LEVITICUS 1:2–4

He did not enter
by means of the blood of goats and calves;
but he entered the Most Holy Place
once for all by his own blood,
having obtained eternal redemption.
The blood of goats and bulls and the ashes of a heifer
    sprinkled on those who are ceremonially unclean
sanctify them so that they are outwardly clean.
How much more then,
will the blood of Christ,
who through the eternal Spirit
    offered himself unblemished to God,
cleanse our consciences from acts that lead to death,
so that we may serve the living God!   HEBREWS 9:12–14

Reconciled to God

God was pleased
>   to have all his fullness dwell in him,
and through him to reconcile to himself all things,
whether things on earth or things in heaven,
by making peace through his blood,
shed on the cross.
Once you were alienated from God
and were enemies in your minds
because of your evil behaviour.
But now he has reconciled you
by Christ's physical body through death
to present you holy in his sight,
without blemish and free from accusation.

COLOSSIANS 1:19–22

Therefore, if anyone is in Christ,
he is a new creation;
the old has gone, the new has come!
All this is from God,
who reconciled us to himself through Christ
and gave us the ministry of reconciliation:
that God was reconciling the world to himself in Christ,
not counting men's sins against them.
And he has committed to us
the message of reconciliation.
We are therefore Christ's ambassadors,
as though God were making his appeal through us –
we implore you on Christ's behalf:
Be reconciled to God.   2 CORINTHIANS 5:17–20

After three days

Mary Magdalene,
Mary the mother of James, and Salome
bought spices so that they might go
    to anoint Jesus' body.
Very early on the first day of the week,
just after sunrise,
they were on their way to the tomb
and they asked each other,
'Who will roll the stone away
    from the entrance of the tomb?'
But when they looked up,
they saw that the stone, which was very large,
    had been rolled away.
As they entered the tomb,
they saw a young man dressed in a white robe
    sitting on the right side,
and they were alarmed.
'Don't be alarmed,' he said.
'You are looking for Jesus the Nazarene,
who was crucified.
He has risen! He is not here.'   MARK 16:1–6

A woman giving birth to a child has pain
because her time has come;
but when her baby is born
she forgets the anguish
because of her joy that a child
    is born into the world.
So with you:
Now is your time of grief,
but I will see you again and you will rejoice,
and no-one will take away your joy.   JOHN 16:21,22

We ate and drank with him!

Jesus himself stood among them
and said to them,
'Peace be with you.'
They were startled and frightened,
thinking they saw a ghost.
He showed them his hands and feet.
And while they still did not believe it
because of joy and amazement,
he asked them,
'Do you have anything here to eat?'
They gave him a piece of broiled fish,
and he took it and ate it in their presence.
He said to them,
'This is what I told you while I was still with you:
Everything must be fulfilled that is written about me
     in the Law of Moses,
the Prophets and the Psalms.'   LUKE 24:36,37,40–44

Then Peter began to speak:
'We are witnesses of everything Jesus did
     in the country of the Jews and in Jerusalem.
They killed him by hanging him on a tree,
but God raised him from the dead on the third day
and caused him to be seen.
He was not seen by all the people,
but by witnesses whom God had already chosen –
by us who ate and drank with him
     after he rose from the dead.
All the prophets testify about him
that everyone who believes in him
receives forgiveness of sins through his name.'
        ACTS 10:34,39–41,43

The desolation

Those who passed by hurled insults at him,
shaking their heads and saying,
'So! You who are going to destroy the temple
        and build it in three days,
come down from the cross and save yourself!'
At the sixth hour darkness came over the whole land
        until the ninth hour.
And at the ninth hour Jesus cried out in a loud voice,
'Eloi, Eloi, lama sabachthani?' –
which means,
'My God, my God,
why have you forsaken me?'   MARK 15:29,30,33,34

My God, my God, why have you forsaken me?
Why are you so far from saving me,
so far from the words of my groaning?
O my God, I cry out by day, but you do not answer,
by night, and am not silent.
All who see me mock me;
they hurl insults, shaking their heads:
'He trusts in the Lord; let the Lord rescue him.
Let him deliver him, since he delights in him.'
                            PSALM 22:1,2,7,8

Christ redeemed us from the curse of the law
by becoming a curse for us,
for it is written:
'Cursed is everyone who is hanged on a tree.'   GALATIANS 3:13

The wisdom of God

The chief priests and the teachers of the law
    mocked him among themselves.
'He saved others,' they said,
'but he can't save himself!
Let this Christ, this King of Israel,
come down now from the cross,
that we may see and believe.'   MARK 15:31,32

For the message of the cross
is foolishness to those who are perishing,
but to us who are being saved it is the power of God.
For since in the wisdom of God
the world through its wisdom did not know him,
God was pleased
    through the foolishness of what was preached
to save those who believe.
Jews demand miraculous signs
and Greeks look for wisdom,
but we preach Christ crucified:
a stumbling block to Jews
and foolishness to Gentiles,
but to those whom God has called,
both Jews and Greeks,
Christ the power of God
and the wisdom of God.   1 CORINTHIANS 1:18,21–24

Into the presence of God

It was now about the sixth hour,
and darkness came over the whole land
    until the ninth hour;
for the sun stopped shining.
And the curtain of the temple
    was torn in two.   LUKE 23:44,45

Therefore, brothers,
since we have confidence to enter the Most Holy Place
by the blood of Jesus,
by the new and living way opened for us
    through the curtain,
that is, his body,
and since we have a great priest
over the house of God,
let us draw near to God with a sincere heart
in full assurance of faith,
having our hearts sprinkled
    to cleanse us from a guilty conscience
and having our bodies washed with pure water.
         HEBREWS 10:19–22

In Christ and through faith in him
we may approach God with freedom and confidence.
         EPHESIANS 3:12

The great high priest

And when Jesus had cried out again in a loud voice,
he gave up his spirit.
At that moment
the curtain of the temple was torn in two
    from top to bottom.   MATTHEW 27:50,51

For the generations to come
this burnt offering is to be made regularly
at the entrance to the Tent of Meeting
    before the Lord.
There I will meet you and speak to you;
there also I will meet with the Israelites,
and the place will be consecrated by my glory.
So I will consecrate the Tent of Meeting and the altar
and will consecrate Aaron and his sons
    to serve me as priests.
Then I will dwell among the Israelites and be their God.
They will know that I am the Lord their God,
who brought them out of Egypt
so that I might dwell among them.
I am the Lord their God.   EXODUS 29:42–47

Therefore, since we have a great high priest
who has gone through the heavens,
Jesus the Son of God,
let us hold firmly to the faith we profess.
For we do not have a high priest
who is unable to sympathise with our weaknesses,
but we have one who has been tempted in every way,
just as we are – yet was without sin.
Let us then approach the throne of grace
    with confidence,
so that we may receive mercy
and find grace to help us in our time of need.
      HEBREWS 4:14–16

For all to see

When the centurion and those with him
    who were guarding Jesus
saw the earthquake and all that had happened,
they were terrified, and exclaimed,
'Surely he was the Son of God!'   MATTHEW 27:54

Jesus said,
'When you have lifted up the Son of Man,
then you will know who I am
and that I do nothing on my own
but speak just what the Father has taught me.
The one who sent me is with me;
he has not left me alone,
for I always do what pleases him.'
Even as he spoke,
many put their faith in him.   JOHN 8:28–30

God forgave us all our sins,
having cancelled the written code,
    with its regulations,
that was against us and that stood opposed to us;
he took it away, nailing it to the cross.
And having disarmed the powers and authorities,
he made a public spectacle of them,
triumphing over them by the cross.   COLOSSIANS 2:13–15

The only sacrifice for sin

These are the regulations for the sin offering:
The sin offering is to be slaughtered before the Lord
in the place where the burnt offering is slaughtered;
it is most holy.
Whatever touches any of the flesh will become holy. . .

LEVITICUS 6:25,27

You know that it was not with perishable things
such as silver or gold
that you were redeemed from the empty way of life
    handed down to you from your forefathers,
but with the precious blood of Christ,
a lamb without blemish or defect.
Through him you believed in God,
who raised him from the dead and glorified him,
and so your faith and hope are in God.   1 PETER 1:18,19,21

'Worthy is the Lamb, who was slain,
to receive power and wealth and wisdom and strength
    and honour and glory and praise!
To him who sits on the throne and to the Lamb
be praise and honour and glory and power
    for ever and ever!'   REVELATION 5:12,13

John saw Jesus coming towards him and said,
'Look, the Lamb of God,
who takes away the sin of the world!'   JOHN 1:29

The terrible sacrilege

They came to a place called Golgotha
(which means The Place of the Skull).
There they offered him wine to drink,
    mixed with gall;
but after tasting it, he refused to drink it.
When they had crucified him,
they divided up his clothes by casting lots.
And sitting down, they kept watch over him there.
Above his head
they placed the written charge against him:
THIS IS JESUS, THE KING OF THE JEWS.
Two robbers were crucified with him,
one on his right and one on his left.   MATTHEW 27:33–38

I am poured out like water,
and all my bones are out of joint.
My heart has turned to wax;
it has melted away within me.
My strength is dried up like a potsherd,
and my tongue sticks to the roof of my mouth;
you lay me in the dust of death.
Dogs have surrounded me;
a band of evil men has encircled me,
they have pierced my hands and my feet.
I can count all my bones;
people stare and gloat over me.
They divide my garments among them
and cast lots for my clothing.   PSALM 22:14–18

The interrogators

Herod plied Jesus with many questions,
but Jesus gave him no answer.
The chief priests and the teachers of the law
     were standing there,
vehemently accusing him.
Then Herod and his soldiers ridiculed and mocked him.
Dressing him in an elegant robe,
they sent him back to Pilate.
That day Herod and Pilate became friends –
before this they had been enemies.   LUKE 23:9–12

Herod and Pontius Pilate
met together with the Gentiles and the people of Israel
     in this city
to conspire against your holy servant Jesus,
     whom you anointed.
They did what your power and will
had decided beforehand should happen.   ACTS 4:27,28

'Where do you come from?'
Pilate asked Jesus,
but Jesus gave him no answer.
'Do you refuse to speak to me?' Pilate said.
'Don't you realise I have power
either to free you or to crucify you?'
Jesus answered,
'You would have no power over me
if it were not given to you from above.
Therefore the one who handed me over to you
is guilty of a greater sin.'   JOHN 19:9–11

Testifying to the truth

Pilate then went back inside the palace,
summoned Jesus and asked him,
'Are you the king of the Jews?'
'Is that your own idea,' Jesus asked,
'or did others talk to you about me?'
'Do you think I am a Jew?' Pilate replied,
'It was your people and your chief priests
    who handed you over to me.
What is it you have done?'
Jesus said, 'My kingdom is not of this world.
If it were, my servants would fight
    to prevent my arrest by the Jews.
But now my kingdom is from another place.'
'You are a king, then!' said Pilate.
Jesus answered, 'You are right in saying
    that I am a king.
In fact, for this reason I was born,
and for this I came into the world,
to testify to the truth.
Everyone on the side of truth listens to me.'   JOHN 18:33–37

In the sight of God,
who gives life to everything,
and of Christ Jesus,
who while testifying before Pontius Pilate
    made the good confession,
I charge you to keep this commandment
without spot or blame
until the appearing of our Lord Jesus Christ.

1 TIMOTHY 6:13,14

The great injustice

'Do you want me to release to you
the king of the Jews?' asked Pilate,
knowing it was out of envy
that the chief priests had handed Jesus over to him.
But the chief priests stirred up the crowd
    to have Pilate release Barabbas instead.
'What shall I do, then,
with the one you call the king of the Jews?'
Pilate asked them.
'Crucify him!' they shouted.
'Why? What crime has he committed?'
    asked Pilate.
But they shouted all the louder,
'Crucify him!'
Wanting to satisfy the crowd,
Pilate released Barabbas to them.
He had Jesus flogged,
and handed him over to be crucified.   MARK 15:9–15

Do not spread false reports.
Do not help a wicked man
by being a malicious witness.
Do not follow the crowd in doing wrong.
When you give testimony in a lawsuit,
do not pervert justice by siding with the crowd.
Do not deny justice to your poor people
    in their lawsuits.
Have nothing to do with a false charge
and do not put an innocent or honest person to death,
for I will not acquit the guilty.
Do not accept a bribe,
for a bribe blinds those who see
and twists the words of the righteous.   EXODUS 23:1,2,6–8

The humility and the humiliation

The high priest tore his clothes.
'Why do we need any more witnesses?' he asked.
'You have heard the blasphemy.
What do you think?'
They all condemned him as worthy of death.
Then some began to spit at him;
they blindfolded him,
struck him with their fists,
and said, 'Prophesy!'
And the guards took him and beat him.   MARK 14:63–65

I offered my back to those who beat me,
my cheeks to those who pulled out my beard;
I did not hide my face from mocking and spitting.

                                              ISAIAH 50:6

Then Pilate released Barabbas to the people.
But he had Jesus flogged,
and handed him over to be crucified.
Then the governor's soldiers took Jesus
      into the Praetorium
and gathered the whole company of soldiers around him.
They stripped him and put a scarlet robe on him,
and then wove a crown of thorns
and set it on his head.
They put a staff in his right hand
and knelt in front of him and mocked him.
'Hail, King of the Jews!' they said.
They spat on him,
and took the staff and struck him on the head
      again and again.   MATTHEW 27:26–30

Betraying Jesus

Even my close friend, whom I trusted,
he who shared my bread,
has lifted up his heel against me.   PSALM 41:9

When evening came,
Jesus arrived with the Twelve.
While they were reclining at the table eating, he said,
'I tell you the truth, one of you will betray me –
one who is eating with me.'
They were saddened,
and one by one they said to him,
'Surely not I?'
'It is one of the Twelve,' he replied,
'one who dips bread into the bowl with me.
The Son of Man will go just as it is written about him.
But woe to that man who betrays the Son of Man!
It would be better for him
if he had not been born.'   MARK 14:17–21

As soon as Judas took the bread,
Satan entered into him.
'What you are about to do, do quickly,'
    Jesus told him,
but no-one at the meal
    understood why Jesus said this to him.
As soon as Judas had taken the bread,
he went out.
And it was night.   JOHN 13:27,28,30

The agonizing decision

Jesus withdrew about a stone's throw beyond them,
knelt down and prayed,
'Father, if you are willing,
take this cup from me;
yet not my will, but yours be done.' LUKE 22:41,42

Again and again
they struck him on the head with a staff
    and spat on him.
Falling on their knees, they worshipped him.
And when they had mocked him,
they took off the purple robe
and put his own clothes on him.
Then they led him out to crucify him. MARK 15:19,20

Surely he took up our infirmities
and carried our sorrows,
yet we considered him stricken by God,
smitten by him, and afflicted.
But he was pierced for our transgressions,
he was crushed for our iniquities;
the punishment that brought us peace was upon him,
and by his wounds we are healed.
We all, like sheep, have gone astray,
each of us has turned to his own way
and the Lord has laid on him
the iniquity of us all. ISAIAH 53:4–6

He himself bore our sins in his body on the tree,
so that we might die to sins
    and live for righteousness;
by his wounds you have been healed. 1 PETER 2:24

The path of obedience

Yet it was the Lord's will to crush him
and cause him to suffer,
and though the Lord makes his life a guilt offering,
he will see his offspring and prolong his days,
and the will of the Lord will prosper in his hand.
After the suffering of his soul,
he will see the light of life and be satisfied
by his knowledge my righteous servant will justify many,
and he will bear their iniquities.
Therefore I will give him a portion among the great,
and he will divide the spoils with the strong,
because he poured out his life unto death,
and was numbered with the transgressors.
For he bore the sin of many,
and made intercession for the transgressors.   ISAIAH 53:10–12

And being found in appearance as a man,
he humbled himself and became obedient to death –
even death on a cross!
Therefore God exalted him to the highest place
and gave him the name that is above every name,
that at the name of Jesus every knee should bow,
in heaven and on earth and under the earth,
and every tongue confess that Jesus Christ is Lord,
to the glory of God the Father.   PHILIPPIANS 2:8–11

Judas betrays Jesus

My companion attacks his friends;
he violates his covenant.
His speech is smooth as butter,
yet war is in his heart;
his words are more soothing than oil,
yet they are drawn swords.   PSALM 55:20,21

Just as Jesus was speaking,
Judas, one of the Twelve, appeared.
With him was a crowd armed with swords and clubs,
sent from the chief priests,
    the teachers of the law and the elders.
Now the betrayer had arranged a signal with them:
'The one I kiss is the man;
arrest him and lead him away under guard.'
Going at once to Jesus,
Judas said, 'Rabbi!' and kissed him.
The men seized Jesus and arrested him.
Then one of those standing near drew his sword
and struck the servant of the high priest,
    cutting off his ear.
'Am I leading a rebellion,' said Jesus,
'that you have come out with swords and clubs
    to capture me?
Every day I was with you,
teaching in the temple courts,
and you did not arrest me.
But the Scriptures must be fulfilled.'
Then everyone deserted him and fled.   MARK 14:43–50

Peter's experience

As soon as Simon Peter heard him say,
'It is the Lord,'
he wrapped his outer garment around him
and jumped into the water.
The other disciples followed in the boat,
towing the net full of fish. . .
Jesus said to them,
'Come and have breakfast.'
None of the disciples dared ask him,
'Who are you?'
They knew it was the Lord.   JOHN 21:7,8,12

For what I received I passed on to you
        as of first importance:
that Christ died for our sins
according to the Scriptures,
that he was buried,
that he was raised on the third day
according to the Scriptures,
and that he appeared to Peter,
and then to the Twelve.
After that,
he appeared to more than five hundred
        of the brothers at the same time.   1 CORINTHIANS 15:3–6

Praise be to the God and Father
        of our Lord Jesus Christ!
In his great mercy he has given us new birth
into a living hope through the resurrection
        of Jesus Christ from the dead,
and into an inheritance that can never perish,
spoil or fade.   1 PETER 1:3,4

In the twinkling of an eye

Listen, I tell you a mystery:
We will not all sleep, but we will all be changed –
in a flash, in the twinkling of an eye,
at the last trumpet.
For the trumpet will sound,
the dead will be raised imperishable,
and we will be changed.
For the perishable must clothe itself
    with the imperishable,
and the mortal with immortality.
When the perishable has been clothed
    with the imperishable,
and the mortal with immortality,
then the saying that is written will come true:
'Death has been swallowed up in victory.'
'Where, O death, is your victory?
Where, O death, is your sting?'
The sting of death is sin,
and the power of sin is the law.
But thanks be to God!
He gives us the victory
through our Lord Jesus Christ.   1 CORINTHIANS 15:51–57

Brothers, we do not want you to be ignorant
about those who fall asleep,
or to grieve like the rest of men, who have no hope.
We believe that Jesus died and rose again
and so we believe that God will bring with Jesus
    those who have fallen asleep in him.
And so we will be with the Lord for ever.
Therefore encourage each other
    with these words.   1 THESSALONIANS 4:13,14,17,18

Our hope in Christ

Do not let your hearts be troubled.
Trust in God; trust also in me.
In my Father's house are many rooms;
if it were not so, I would have told you.
I am going there to prepare a place for you.
And if I go and prepare a place for you,
I will come back and take you to be with me
that you also may be where I am.   JOHN 14:1-3

We know that the one
who raised the Lord Jesus from the dead
will also raise us with Jesus
and will bring us with you in his presence.
All this is for your benefit,
so that the grace that is reaching
      more and more people
may cause thanksgiving to overflow
to the glory of God.
Therefore we do not lose heart.
Though outwardly we are wasting away,
yet inwardly we are being renewed day by day.
                          2 CORINTHIANS 4:14-16

Praise be to the God and Father
      of our Lord Jesus Christ!
In his great mercy
he has given us new birth into a living hope
through the resurrection of Jesus Christ
      from the dead,
and into an inheritance
that can never perish, spoil or fade –
kept in heaven for you,
who through faith are shielded by God's power
until the coming of salvation
that is ready to be revealed in the last time.
                          1 PETER 1:4,5

Being raised to life

All that the Father gives me
    will come to me,
and whoever comes to me I will never drive away.
For I have come down from heaven not to do my will
but to do the will of him who sent me.
And this is the will of him who sent me,
that I shall lose none of all that he has given me,
but raise them up at the last day.
For my Father's will
    is that everyone who looks to the Son
and believes in him
shall have eternal life,
and I will raise him up at the last day.   JOHN 6:37–40

When you were dead in your sins
and in the uncircumcision of your sinful nature,
God made you alive with Christ.
He forgave us all our sins,
having cancelled the written code,
with its regulations,
that was against us and that stood opposed to us;
he took it away, nailing it to the cross.   COLOSSIANS 2:13,14

Jesus said to Martha,
'I am the resurrection and the life.
He who believes in me will live,
even though he dies;
and whoever lives and believes in me
will never die.'   JOHN 11:25,26

He has not left us alone!

They urged him strongly,
'Stay with us, for it is nearly evening;
the day is almost over.'
So he went in to stay with them.
When he was at the table with them,
he took bread, gave thanks,
broke it and began to give it to them.
Then their eyes were opened
and they recognised him,
and he disappeared from their sight.   LUKE 24:29–31

I will not leave you as orphans;
I will come to you.
Before long, the world will not see me any more,
but you will see me.
Because I live, you also will live.
On that day you will realise that I am in my Father,
and you are in me, and I am in you.
Whoever has my commands and obeys them,
he is the one who loves me.
He who loves me will be loved by my Father,
and I too will love him
and show myself to him.   JOHN 14:18–21

Again, I tell you
that if two of you on earth
    agree about anything you ask for,
it will be done for you by my Father in heaven.
For where two or three come together in my name,
there am I with them.   MATTHEW 18:19,20

The centrality of the Resurrection

This is the testimony:
God has given us eternal life,
and this life is in his Son.
He who has the Son has life;
he who does not have the Son of God
does not have life.
I write these things to you
who believe in the name of the Son of God
so that you may know that you have eternal life.

1 JOHN 5:11–13

But if it is preached
that Christ has been raised from the dead,
how can some of you say
that there is no resurrection of the dead?
If there is no resurrection of the dead,
then not even Christ has been raised.
And if Christ has not been raised,
our preaching is useless and so is your faith.
For if the dead are not raised,
then Christ has not been raised either.
And if Christ has not been raised,
your faith is futile;
you are still in your sins.
Then those also who have fallen asleep in Christ
      are lost.
If only for this life we have hope in Christ,
we are to be pitied more than all men.
But Christ has indeed been raised from the dead,
the firstfruits of those who have fallen asleep.
For since death came through a man,
the resurrection of the dead comes also through a man.

1 CORINTHIANS 15:12–14,16–21

His is the power

Peter said to them:
'Men of Israel, why does this surprise you?
Why do you stare at us
as if by our own power or godliness
we had made this man walk?
You killed the author of life,
but God raised him from the dead.
We are witnesses of this.
By faith in the name of Jesus,
this man whom you see and know was made strong.
It is Jesus' name and the faith that comes through him
that has given this complete healing to him,
as you can all see.'   ACTS 3:12,15,16

I pray also
that the eyes of your heart may be enlightened
in order that you may know the hope
     to which he has called you,
the riches of his glorious inheritance in the saints,
and his incomparably great power for us who believe.
That power is like the working of his mighty strength,
which he exerted in Christ
when he raised him from the dead
and seated him at his right hand
     in the heavenly realms,
far above all rule and authority,
     power and dominion,
and every title that can be given,
not only in the present age
but also in the one to come.
And God placed all things under his feet
and appointed him to be head over everything
     for the church.   EPHESIANS 1:18–22

He has set us free!

Some sat in darkness and the deepest gloom,
prisoners suffering in iron chains.
Then they cried to the Lord in their trouble,
and he saved them from their distress.
He brought them out of the darkness
    and the deepest gloom
and broke away their chains.
Let them give thanks to the Lord for his unfailing love
and his wonderful deeds for men,
for he breaks down gates of bronze
and cuts through bars of iron.   PSALM 107:10,13–16

Peter was kept in prison,
but the church was earnestly praying to God for him.
The night before Herod was to bring him to trial,
Peter was sleeping between two soldiers,
bound with two chains,
and sentries stood guard at the entrance.
Suddenly an angel of the Lord appeared
and a light shone in the cell.
He struck Peter on the side and woke him up.
'Quick, get up!' he said,
and the chains fell off Peter's wrists.
Peter followed him out of the prison,
but he had no idea
that what the angel was doing was really happening;
he thought he was seeing a vision.
They passed the first and second guards
and came to the iron gate leading to the city.
It opened for them by itself,
and they went through it.   ACTS 12:5–7,9,10

The discovery

The kingdom of heaven
is like treasure hidden in a field.
When a man found it, he hid it again,
and then in his joy went and sold all he had
and bought that field.
Again,
the kingdom of heaven
is like a merchant looking for fine pearls.
When he found one of great value,
he went away and sold everything he had
and bought it. MATTHEW 13:44–46

But whatever was to my profit
I now consider loss for the sake of Christ.
What is more, I consider everything a loss
compared to the surpassing greatness
    of knowing Christ Jesus my Lord,
for whose sake I have lost all things.
I consider them rubbish,
that I may gain Christ and be found in him,
not having a righteousness of my own
    that comes from the law,
but that which is through faith in Christ –
the righteousness that comes from God
    and is by faith.
I want to know Christ
and the power of his resurrection
and the fellowship of sharing in his sufferings,
becoming like him in his death,
and so, somehow,
to attain to the resurrection from the dead.
PHILIPPIANS 3:7–11

Our weakness and God's power

When he came to his senses, he said,
'. . . I will set out and go back to my father
and say to him:
Father,
I have sinned against heaven
and against you.
I am no longer worthy to be called your son. . . '
But while he was still a long way off,
his father saw him and was filled
    with compassion for him;
he ran to his son,
threw his arms around him and kissed him.   LUKE 15:17,18,19,20

Do good to your servant
according to your word, O Lord.
Teach me knowledge and good judgement,
for I believe in your commands.
Before I was afflicted I went astray,
but now I obey your word.
You are good, and what you do is good;
teach me your decrees.
It was good for me to be afflicted
so that I might learn your decrees.   PSALM 119:65– 68,71

In the gospel
a righteousness from God is revealed,
a righteousness that is by faith from first to last,
just as it is written:
'The righteous will live by faith.'   ROMANS 1:17

His grace, not our merit

When the kindness and love
    of God our Saviour appeared,
he saved us,
not because of righteous things we had done,
but because of his mercy. . .   TITUS 3:4,5

The Pharisee stood up and prayed about himself:
'God, I thank you that I am not like all other men –
robbers, evildoers, adulterers –
or even like this tax collector.
I fast twice a week and give a tenth of all I get.'
But the tax collector stood at a distance.
He would not even look up to heaven,
but beat his breast and said,
'God, have mercy on me, a sinner.'
I tell you that this man, rather than the other,
went home justified before God. . .   LUKE 18:11–14

For it is by grace you have been saved,
through faith –
and this not from yourselves,
it is the gift of God –
not by works, so that no-one can boast.
For we are God's workmanship,
created in Christ Jesus to do good works,
which God prepared in advance for us to do.
                                        EPHESIANS 2:8–10

Not to us, O Lord, not to us
    but to your name be the glory,
because of your love and faithfulness.   PSALM 115:1

Confessing our faith in public

If you confess with your mouth, 'Jesus is Lord,'
and believe in your heart
that God raised him from the dead,
you will be saved.
For it is with your heart that you believe
    and are justified,
and it is with your mouth that you confess
    and are saved.   ROMANS 10:9,10

Whoever acknowledges me before men,
I will also acknowledge him
    before my Father in heaven.
But whoever disowns me before men,
I will disown him
    before my Father in heaven.   MATTHEW 10:32,33

Here is a trustworthy saying:
If we died with him, we will also live with him;
if we endure, we will also reign with him.
If we disown him, he will also disown us;
if we are faithless, he will remain faithful,
for he cannot disown himself.   2 TIMOTHY 2:11–13

Come and listen, all you who fear God;
let me tell you what he has done for me.
I cried out to him with my mouth;
his praise was on my tongue.
If I had cherished sin in my heart,
the Lord would not have listened;
but God has surely listened
and heard my voice in prayer.
Praise be to God, who has not rejected my prayer
or withheld his love from me!   PSALM 66:16–20

Coming to faith in humility

At that time Jesus,
full of joy through the Holy Spirit, said,
'I praise you, Father,
Lord of heaven and earth,
because you have hidden these things
    from the wise and learned,
and revealed them to little children.
Yes, Father, for this was your good pleasure.'   LUKE 10:21

But when the chief priests and the teachers of the law
    saw the wonderful things he did
and the children shouting in the temple area,
    'Hosanna to the Son of David,'
they were indignant.
'Do you hear what these children are saying?'
    they asked him.
'Yes,' replied Jesus, 'have you never read,
"From the lips of children and infants,
you have ordained praise"?'   MATTHEW 21:15,16

People were bringing little children to Jesus
to have him touch them,
but the disciples rebuked them.
When Jesus saw this, he was indignant.
He said to them,
'Let the little children come to me,
and do not hinder them,
for the kingdom of God belongs to such as these.
I tell you the truth,
anyone who will not receive the kingdom of God
    like a little child
will never enter it.'   MARK 10:13–15

The outsiders

Naaman was commander of the army
    of the king of Aram. . .
He was a valiant soldier,
but he had leprosy.
Elisha sent a messenger to say to him,
'Go, wash yourself seven times in the Jordan,
and your flesh will be restored
and you will be cleansed.'
So he went down
and dipped himself in the Jordan seven times,
as the man of God had told him,
and his flesh was restored and became clean
like that of a young boy.
Then Naaman and all his attendants
went back to the man of God.
He stood before him and said,
'Now I know
that there is no God in all the world
except in Israel.'   2 KINGS 5:1,10,14,15

When Jesus had entered Capernaum,
a centurion came to him,
asking for help.
'Lord, I do not deserve
to have you come under my roof.
But just say the word,
and my servant will be healed.'
When Jesus heard this, he was astonished
and said to those following him,
'I tell you the truth,
I have not found anyone in Israel
with such great faith.'   MATTHEW 8:5–8,10

The last will be first

People will come from east and west and north and south,
and will take their places at the feast
in the kingdom of God.
Indeed there are those who are last who will be first,
and first who will be last.   LUKE 13:29,30

When one of those at the table with him heard this,
he said to Jesus,
'Blessed is the man who will eat at the feast
in the kingdom of God.'
Jesus replied:
'A certain man was preparing a great banquet
and invited many guests.
At the time of the banquet he sent his servant
to tell those who had been invited,
"Come, for everything is now ready."
But they all alike began to make excuses. . .
The servant came back and reported this to his master.
Then the owner of the house became angry
and ordered his servant,
"Go out quickly
        into the streets and alleys of the town
and bring in the poor, the crippled,
        the blind and the lame.
I tell you,
not one of those men who were invited
will get a taste of my banquet." '   LUKE 14:15–18,21,24

On this mountain the Lord Almighty will prepare
a feast of rich food for all peoples,
a banquet of aged wine –
the best of meats and the finest of wines.
In that day they will say, 'Surely this is our God;
we trusted in him, and he saved us.
This is the Lord, we trusted in him;
let us rejoice and be glad in his salvation.'   ISAIAH 25:6,9

The inclusion of the Gentiles

Then Peter began to speak:
'I now realise how true it is
that God does not show favouritism
but accepts men from every nation
who fear him and do what is right.   ACTS 10:34,35

Therefore, remember that formerly
you who are Gentiles by birth. . .
were separate from Christ,
excluded from citizenship in Israel
and foreigners to the covenants of the promise,
without hope and without God in the world.
But now in Christ Jesus you who once were far away
have been brought near through the blood of Christ.
For he himself is our peace,
who has made the two one
and has destroyed the barrier,
the dividing wall of hostility,
by abolishing in his flesh
the law with its commandments and regulations.
His purpose was to create in himself
        one new man out of the two,
thus making peace,
and in this one body
to reconcile both of them to God through the cross,
by which he put to death their hostility.
                                    EPHESIANS 2:11,12–16

There is neither Jew nor Greek,
slave nor free, male nor female,
for you are all one in Christ Jesus.
If you belong to Christ,
then you are Abraham's seed,
and heirs according to the promise.   GALATIANS 3:28,29

Trust in the Lord – do not be afraid

Moses answered the people,
'Do not be afraid.
Stand firm and you will see
the deliverance the Lord will bring you today. . . '
Then the Lord said to Moses,
'Why are you crying out to me?
Tell the Israelites to move on.
Raise your staff
and stretch out your hand over the sea
    to divide the water
so that the Israelites can go through the sea
on dry ground.
I will harden the hearts of the Egyptians
so that they will go in after them.'   EXODUS 14:13,15–17

The Lord is my light and my salvation –
whom shall I fear?
The Lord is the stronghold of my life –
of whom shall I be afraid?
When evil men advance against me to devour my flesh,
when my enemies and my foes attack me,
they will stumble and fall.
Though an army besiege me,
my heart will not fear;
though war break out against me,
even then will I be confident.   PSALM 27:1–3

Trust in the Lord who cares for you

After Job had prayed for his friends,
the Lord made him prosperous again
and gave him twice as much as he had before.
The Lord blessed the latter part of Job's life
more than the first.   JOB 42:10,12

Trust in the Lord with all your heart
and lean not on your own understanding;
in all your ways acknowledge him,
and he will make your paths straight.
Do not be wise in your own eyes;
fear the Lord and shun evil.
This will bring health to your body
and nourishment to your bones.
Honour the Lord with your wealth,
with the firstfruits of all your crops;
then your barns will be filled to overflowing,
and your vats will brim over with new wine.
                                PROVERBS 3:5–10

Whoever would love life and see good days
must keep his tongue from evil
and his lips from deceitful speech.
He must turn from evil and do good;
he must seek peace and pursue it.
For the eyes of the Lord are on the righteous
and his ears are attentive to their prayer,
but the face of the Lord is against those
    who do evil.   1 PETER 3:10–12

The God who provides

'As surely as the Lord your God lives,'
she replied,
'I don't have any bread –
only a handful of flour in a jar
and a little oil in a jug. . . '
Elijah said to her, 'Don't be afraid. . .
For this is what the Lord, the God of Israel says:
"The jar of flour will not be used up
and the jug of oil will not run dry
until the day the Lord gives rain on the land." '

1 KINGS 17:12,13,14

Andrew, Simon Peter's brother, spoke up,
'Here is a boy with five small barley loaves
        and two small fish,
but how far will they go among so many?'
Jesus then took the loaves, gave thanks,
and distributed to those who were seated
as much as they wanted.
He did the same with the fish.

JOHN 6:8,9,11

Some wandered in desert wastelands,
finding no way to a city where they could settle.
They were hungry and thirsty,
and their lives ebbed away.
Then they cried out to the Lord in their trouble,
and he delivered them from their distress.
Let them give thanks to the Lord
        for his unfailing love
and his wonderful deeds for men,
for he satisfies the thirsty
and fills the hungry with good things.

PSALM 107:4–6,8,9

God meets all our needs

Trust in the Lord and do good;
dwell in the land and enjoy safe pasture.
Delight yourself in the Lord
and he will give you the desires of your heart.
Commit your way to the Lord;
trust in him and he will do this:
He will make your righteousness
    shine like the dawn,
the justice of your cause
    like the noonday sun.
Be still before the Lord
and wait patiently for him;
do not fret when men succeed in their ways,
when they carry out their wicked schemes.
Refrain from anger and turn from wrath;
do not fret – it leads only to evil.   PSALM 37:3–8

So do not worry, saying,
'What shall we eat?'
or 'What shall we drink?'
or 'What shall we wear?'
For the pagans run after all these things,
and your heavenly Father knows that you need them.
But seek first his kingdom
    and his righteousness,
and all these things
will be given to you as well.
Therefore do not worry about tomorrow,
for tomorrow will worry about itself.
Each day has enough trouble of its own.   MATTHEW 6:31–34

The God who satisfies

Two things I ask of you, O Lord;
do not refuse me before I die:
Keep falsehood and lies far from me;
give me neither poverty nor riches,
but give me only my daily bread.
Otherwise, I may have too much and disown you
and say, 'Who is the Lord?'
Or I may become poor and steal,
and so dishonour the name of my God.   PROVERBS 30:7–9

Moses said to them,
'It is the bread the Lord has given you to eat.
This is what the Lord has commanded:
"Each one is to gather as much as he needs. . . "
No one is to keep any of it until morning.'
However, some of them paid no attention to Moses;
they kept part of it until morning,
but it was full of maggots and began to smell.
So Moses was angry with them.   EXODUS 16:15,16,19,20

I have learned to be content
     whatever the circumstances.
I know what it is to be in need,
and I know what it is to have plenty.
I have learned the secret of being content
in any and every situation,
whether well fed or hungry,
whether living in plenty or in want.
I can do everything
through him who gives me strength.   PHILIPPIANS 4:11–13

The protection of God

She got a papyrus basket for him
and coated it with tar and pitch.
Then she placed the child in it
and put it among the reeds
     along the bank of the Nile.
Then Pharaoh's daughter
went down to the Nile to bathe,
and her attendants were walking
     along the river bank.
She saw the basket among the reeds
and sent her slave girl to get it.
She opened it and saw the baby. . .
When the child grew older . . . he became her son.
She named him Moses, saying,
'I drew him out of the water.'   EXODUS 2:3,5,6,10

You brought me out of the womb;
you made me trust in you
even at my mother's breast.
From birth I was cast upon you;
from my mother's womb
you have been my God.
Do not be far from me,
for trouble is near
and there is no-one to help.   PSALM 22:9–11

An angel of the Lord appeared to Joseph in a dream.
'Get up,' he said, 'take the child and his mother
and escape to Egypt.
Stay there until I tell you,
for Herod is going to search for the child
to kill him.'   MATTHEW 2:13

The God who defends us

Are not two sparrows sold for a penny?
Yet not one of them will fall to the ground
    apart from the will of your Father.
And even the very hairs of your head
are all numbered.
So don't be afraid;
you are worth more than many sparrows.   MATTHEW 10:29–31

The Lord watches over you –
the Lord is your shade at your right hand;
the sun will not harm you by day,
nor the moon by night.
The Lord will keep you from all harm –
he will watch over your life.   PSALM 121:5–7

He who sits on the throne
will spread his tent over them.
Never again will they hunger;
never again will they thirst.
The sun will not beat upon them,
nor any scorching heat.
For the Lamb at the centre of the throne
will be their shepherd;
he will lead them to springs of living water.
And God will wipe away
every tear from their eyes.   REVELATION 7:15–17

They will feed beside the roads
and find pasture on every barren hill.
They will neither hunger nor thirst,
nor will the desert heat or the sun beat upon them.
He who has compassion on them will guide them
and lead them beside springs of water.   ISAIAH 49:9,10

God cares for the humble

Then Hannah prayed and said:
'My heart rejoices in the Lord;
in the Lord my horn is lifted high. . .
There is no-one holy like the Lord;
there is no-one besides you;
there is no Rock like our God.
Do not keep talking so proudly
or let your mouth speak such arrogance,
for the Lord is a God who knows,
and by him deeds are weighed.
The Lord brings death and makes alive;
he brings down to the grave
and raises up.'   1 SAMUEL 2:1–3,6

And Mary said:
'My soul praises the Lord
and my spirit rejoices in God my Saviour,
for he has been mindful of the humble state
    of his servant.
From now on all generations will call me blessed,
for the Mighty One has done great things for me –
holy is his name.
His mercy extends to those who fear him,
from generation to generation.
He has performed mighty deeds with his arm;
he has scattered those who are proud
    in their inmost thoughts.
He has brought down rulers from their thrones
but has lifted up the humble.
He has filled the hungry with good things
but has sent the rich away empty.'   LUKE 1:46–53

God is faithful

I proclaimed a fast,
so that we might humble ourselves before our God
and ask him for a safe journey for us
and our children, with all our possessions.
I was ashamed to ask the king
for soldiers and horsemen to protect us
        from enemies on the road,
because we had told the king;
'The good hand of our God
is on everyone who looks to him,
but his great anger
is against all who forsake him.'
So we fasted and petitioned our God about this,
and he answered our prayer.   EZRA 8:21–23

For the Lord God is a sun and shield;
the Lord bestows favour and honour;
no good thing does he withold
from those whose walk is blameless.
O Lord Almighty,
blessed is the man who trusts in you.   PSALM 84:11,12

And we know that in all things God works
for the good of those who love him,
who have been called according to his purpose.
For those God foreknew he also predestined
to be conformed to the likeness of his Son,
that he might be the firstborn among many brothers.
And those he predestined, he also called;
those he called, he also justified;
those he justified, he also glorified.   ROMANS 8:28–30

His constant love

Ruth carried the barley back to town,
and her mother-in-law saw how much she had gathered.
Ruth also brought out and gave her
what she had left over
after she had eaten enough.
Her mother-in-law asked her,
'Where did you glean today? Where did you work?
Blessed be the man who took notice of you!'
Then Ruth told her mother-in-law. . .
'The name of the man I worked with today is Boaz.'
'The Lord bless him!'
Naomi said to her daughter-in-law.
'The Lord has not stopped showing his kindness
to the living and the dead.'   RUTH 2:18,19,20

How priceless is your unfailing love!
Both high and low among men
find refuge in the shadow of your wings.
They feast on the abundance of your house;
you give them drink from your river of delights.
For with you is the fountain of life;
in your light we see light.
Continue your love to those who know you,
your righteousness to the upright in heart.
May the foot of the proud not come against me,
nor the hand of the wicked drive me away.
See how the evildoers lie fallen –
thrown down, not able to rise!   PSALM 36:7–12

He satisfies the thirsty

Come, all you who are thirsty,
come to the waters;
and you who have no money, come, buy and eat!
Come, buy wine and milk without money
and without cost.
Why spend money on what is not bread,
and your labour on what does not satisfy?
Listen, listen to me, and eat what is good,
and your soul will delight in the richest of fare.
Give ear and come to me;
hear me, that your soul may live.   ISAIAH 55:1–3

If you knew the gift of God
and who it is that asks you for a drink,
you would have asked him
and he would have given you living water.
Everyone who drinks this water
will be thirsty again,
but whoever drinks the water I give him
will never thirst.
Indeed, the water I give him
will become in him
a spring of water
welling up to eternal life.   JOHN 4:10,13,14

To him who is thirsty
I will give to drink without cost
from the spring of the water of life.
He who overcomes will inherit all this,
and I will be his God
and he will be my son.   REVELATION 21:6,7

Jesus our shepherd

The Lord is my shepherd,
I shall lack nothing.
Even though I walk
through the valley of the shadow of death,
I will fear no evil, for you are with me;
your rod and staff, they comfort me.   PSALM 23:1,4

He tends his flock like a shepherd:
He gathers the lambs in his arms
and carries them close to his heart;
he gently leads those that have young.   ISAIAH 40:11

For this is what the Sovereign Lord says:
I myself will search for my sheep
and look after them.
I will search for the lost and bring back the strays.
I will bind up the injured
and strengthen the weak. . .   EZEKIEL 34:11,16

I am the good shepherd;
I know my sheep
and my sheep know me –
just as the Father knows me
and I know the Father –
and I lay down my life for the sheep.   JOHN 10:14,15

For you were like sheep going astray,
but now you have returned
to the Shepherd and Overseer of your souls.   1 PETER 2:25

The future hope

Your eyes will see Jerusalem,
a peaceful abode, a tent that will not be moved;
its stakes will never be pulled up,
nor any of its ropes broken.
There the Lord will be our Mighty One.
It will be like a place of broad rivers
    and streams. . .
The Lord is our king,
it is he who will save us.
No-one living in Zion will say, 'I am ill';
and the sins of those who dwell there
will be forgiven.   ISAIAH 33:20,21,22,24

Then I saw a new heaven and a new earth,
for the first heaven and the first earth
had passed away,
and there was no longer any sea.
I saw the Holy City, the new Jerusalem,
coming down out of heaven from God,
prepared as a bride
beautifully dressed for her husband.
And I heard a loud voice from the throne saying,
'Now the dwelling of God is with men,
and he will live with them.
They will be his people,
and God himself will be with them and be their God.'
He said to me: 'It is done.
I am the Alpha and the Omega,
the Beginning and the End.
To him who is thirsty
I will give to drink without cost
from the spring of the water of life.
He who overcomes will inherit all this,
and I will be his God and he will be my son.'
                                    REVELATION 21:1–3,6,7

The exalted Christ

In my vision at night I looked,
and there before me was one like a son of man,
coming with the clouds of heaven.
He approached the Ancient of Days
and was led into his presence.
He was given authority, glory
    and sovereign power;
all peoples, nations
    and men of every language
worshipped him.
His dominion is an everlasting dominion
that will not pass away,
and his kingdom is one that will never be destroyed.

DANIEL 7:13,14

Therefore God exalted him to the highest place
and gave him the name
    that is above every name,
that at the name of Jesus
every knee should bow,
in heaven and on earth
    and under the earth,
and every tongue confess
    that Jesus Christ is Lord,
to the glory of God the Father.   PHILIPPIANS 2:9–11

When they saw Jesus, they worshipped him;
but some doubted.
Then Jesus came to them and said,
'All authority in heaven and on earth
    has been given to me.'   MATTHEW 28:17,18

Christ the heavenly Lord

But in these last days he has spoken to us
    by his Son,
whom he appointed heir of all things,
and through whom he made the universe.
The Son is the radiance of God's glory
and the exact representation of his being,
sustaining all things by his powerful word.
After he had provided purification for sins,
he sat down at the right hand of the Majesty
    in heaven.   HEBREWS 1:2,3

That power is like the working
    of his mighty strength,
which he exerted in Christ
when he raised him from the dead
and seated him at his right hand
    in the heavenly realms,
far above all rule and authority,
power and dominion,
and every title that can be given,
not only in the present age
but also in the one to come.
And God placed all things under his feet
and appointed him to be head over everything
for the church, which is his body,
the fullness of him
who fills everything
    in every way.   EPHESIANS 1:19–23

To him who overcomes,
I will give the right to sit with me on my throne,
just as I overcame
and sat down with my Father on his throne.
                            REVELATION 3:21

The Son, the Spirit and the Father

Beyond all question,
the mystery of godliness is great:
He appeared in a body,
was vindicated by the Spirit,
was seen by angels,
was preached among the nations,
was believed on in the world,
was taken up in glory.   1 TIMOTHY 3:16

Now I am going to him who sent me,
yet none of you asks me,
'Where are you going?'
Because I have said these things,
you are filled with grief.
But I tell you the truth:
It is for your good that I am going away.
Unless I go away,
the Counsellor will not come to you;
but if I go, I will send him to you.
When he comes,
he will convict the world of guilt in regard to sin
and righteousness and judgement:
in regard to sin,
because men do not believe in me;
in regard to righteousness,
because I am going to the Father,
where you can see me no longer;
and in regard to judgement,
because the prince of this world
        now stands condemned.   JOHN 16:5–11

As he went, so he will come again

Jesus was taken up before their very eyes,
and a cloud hid him from their sight.
They were looking intently up into the sky
    as he was going,
when suddenly
two men dressed in white stood beside them.
'Men of Galilee,' they said,
'why do you stand here looking into the sky?
This same Jesus,
who has been taken from you into heaven,
will come back in the same way
    you have seen him go into heaven.'   ACTS 1:9–11

'Behold, I am coming soon!
My reward is with me,
and I will give to everyone
according to what he has done.
I am the Alpha and the Omega,
the First and the Last,
the Beginning and the End.'
The Spirit and the bride say, 'Come!'
And let him who hears say, 'Come!'
He who testifies to these things says,
'Yes, I am coming soon.'
Amen. Come, Lord Jesus.
The grace of the Lord Jesus
    be with God's people.   REVELATION 22:12,13,17,20,21

Our citizenship is in heaven.
And we eagerly await a Saviour from there,
the Lord Jesus Christ.   PHILIPPIANS 3:20

The promise of the Spirit

I will sprinkle clean water on you,
and you will be clean;
I will cleanse you from all your impurities
and from all your idols.
I will give you a new heart
and put a new spirit in you;
I will remove from you your heart of stone
and give you a heart of flesh.
And I will put my Spirit in you
and move you to follow my decrees
and be careful to keep my laws.   EZEKIEL 36:25–27

If you love me, you will obey what I command.
I will ask the Father,
and he will give you another Counsellor
        to be with you for ever –
the Spirit of truth.
The world cannot accept him,
because it neither sees him nor knows him.
But you know him,
for he lives with you and will be in you.   JOHN 14:15–17

This is his command:
to believe in the name of his Son, Jesus Christ,
and to love one another as he commanded us.
Those who obey his commands live in him,
        and he in them.
And this is how we know that he lives in us:
We know it by the Spirit he gave us.   1 JOHN 3:23,24

New birth through the Spirit

In reply Jesus declared,
'I tell you the truth,
unless a man is born again,
he cannot see the kingdom of God.'
'How can a man be born when he is old?'
    Nicodemus asked,
'Surely he cannot enter a second time
into his mother's womb to be born!'
Jesus answered, 'I tell you the truth,
unless a man is born of water and the Spirit,
he cannot enter the kingdom of God.
Flesh gives birth to flesh,
but the Spirit gives birth to spirit.
You should not be surprised at my saying,
"You must be born again."
The wind blows wherever it pleases.
You hear its sound,
but you cannot tell where it comes from
or where it is going.
So it is with everyone born of the Spirit.'   JOHN 3:3–8

God saved us,
not because of righteous things we had done,
but because of his mercy.
He saved us through the washing of rebirth
    and renewal by the Holy Spirit,
whom he poured out on us generously
through Jesus Christ our Saviour,
so that, having been justified by his grace,
we might become heirs
having the hope of eternal life.   TITUS 3:5–7

New life through the Spirit

But if Christ is in you,
your body is dead because of sin,
yet your spirit is alive because of righteousness.
And if the Spirit of him who raised Jesus from the dead
    is living in you,
he who raised Christ from the dead
will also give life to your mortal bodies
    through his Spirit,
who lives in you.
Therefore, brothers, we have an obligation –
but it is not to the sinful nature,
    to live according to it.
For if you live according to the sinful nature,
you will die;
but if by the Spirit
you put to death the misdeeds of the body,
you will live.   ROMANS 8:10–13

Then the Lord said to me,
'Prophesy to these bones and say to them,
"Dry bones,
hear the word of the Lord!
This is what the Sovereign Lord says to these bones:
I will make breath enter you,
and you will come to life. . .
Then you will know that I am the Lord." '   EZEKIEL 37:4,5,6

The work of the Spirit

Those who are led by the Spirit of God
    are sons of God.
For you did not receive a spirit
    that makes you a slave again to fear,
but you received the Spirit of sonship.
And by him we cry, '*Abba*, Father.'
In the same way, the Spirit helps us in our weakness.
We do not know what we ought to pray,
but the Spirit himself intercedes for us
with groans that words cannot express.
And he who searches our hearts
knows the mind of the Spirit,
because the Spirit intercedes for the saints
in accordance with God's will.   ROMANS 8:14,15,26,27

But when he,
The Spirit of truth, comes,
he will guide you into all truth.
He will not speak on his own;
he will speak only what he hears,
and he will tell you what is yet to come.
He will bring glory to me by taking from what is mine
and making it known to you.
All that belongs to the Father is mine.
That is why I said
    the Spirit will take from what is mine
and make it known to you.   JOHN 16:13–15

The power of the Spirit

On the evening of that first day of the week,
when the disciples were together,
with the doors locked for fear of the Jews,
Jesus came and stood among them and said,
'Peace be with you!'
After he said this,
he showed them his hands and side.
The disciples were overjoyed when they saw the Lord.
Again Jesus said, 'Peace be with you!
As the Father has sent me, I am sending you.'
And with that he breathed on them and said,
'Receive the Holy Spirit.
If you forgive anyone his sins, they are forgiven;
if you do not forgive them, they are not forgiven.'

JOHN 20:19–23

On their release,
Peter and John went back to their own people
and reported all that the chief priests and elders
          had said to them.
When they heard this,
they raised their voices together in prayer to God.
'Sovereign Lord,' they said,
'you made the heaven and the earth and the sea,
          and everything in them.
Now, Lord . . . enable your servants
to speak your word with great boldness.
Stretch out your hand to heal
and perform miraculous signs and wonders
through the name of your holy servant Jesus.'
After they prayed,
the place where they were meeting was shaken.
And they were all filled with the Holy Spirit
and spoke the word of God boldly.   ACTS 4:23,24,29–31

Pentecost

This is what the Lord says. . .
I will pour water on the thirsty land,
and streams on the dry ground;
I will pour out my Spirit on your offspring,
and my blessing on your descendants.
One will say, 'I belong to the Lord';
another will call himself by the name of Jacob;
still another will write on his hand, 'The Lord's,'
and will take the name Israel.   ISAIAH 44:2,3,5

When the day of Pentecost came,
they were all together in one place.
Suddenly a sound like the blowing of a violent wind
        came from heaven
and filled the whole house where they were sitting.
They saw what seemed to be tongues of fire
that separated and came to rest on each of them.
All of them were filled with the Holy Spirit
and began to speak in other tongues
        as the Spirit enabled them.   ACTS 2:1–4

Everyone was filled with awe,
and many wonders and miraculous signs
        were done by the apostles.
All the believers were together
and had everything in common.
And the Lord added to their number daily
those who were being saved.   ACTS 2:43,44,47

The fruit of the Spirit

You did not choose me,
but I chose you to go and bear fruit –
fruit that will last.   JOHN 15:16

But the fruit of the Spirit is love, joy, peace,
    patience, kindness, goodness,
    faithfulness, gentleness and self-control.
Against such things there is no law.
Those who belong to Christ Jesus
have crucified the sinful nature
with its passions and desires.
Since we live by the Spirit,
let us keep in step with the Spirit.
Let us not become conceited,
provoking and envying each other.   GALATIANS 5:22–26

Land that drinks in the rain often falling on it
and that produces a crop
    useful to those for whom it is farmed
receives the blessing of God.
But land that produces thorns and thistles
is worthless
and is in danger of being cursed.
In the end it will be burned.
Even though we speak like this, dear friends,
we are confident of better things in your case –
things that accompany salvation.   HEBREWS 6:7–9

The gifts of the Spirit

I will pour out my Spirit on all people.
Your sons and daughters will prophesy,
your old men will dream dreams
your young men will see visions.
Even on my servants, both men and women,
I will pour out my Spirit in those days.   JOEL 2:28,29

To one there is given through the Spirit
     the message of wisdom,
to another the message of knowledge
     by means of the same Spirit,
to another faith by the same Spirit,
to another gifts of healing by that one Spirit,
to another miraculous powers,
to another prophecy,
to another the ability to distinguish between spirits,
to another the ability to speak
     in different kinds of tongues,
and to still another the interpretation of tongues.
All these are the work of one and the same Spirit,
and he gives them to each man,
just as he determines.   1 CORINTHIANS 12:8–11

The sin against the Spirit

Jesus said to the paralytic,
'Son, your sins are forgiven.'
Now some teachers of the law were sitting there,
thinking to themselves,
'Why does this fellow talk like that?
He's blaspheming!
Who can forgive sins but God alone?'
Immediately Jesus knew in his spirit
that this was what they were thinking
    in their hearts. . .   MARK 2:5–8

Then they brought him a demon-possessed man
who was blind and dumb,
and Jesus healed him,
so that he could both talk and see.
But when the Pharisees heard this, they said,
'It is only by Beelzebub the prince of demons,
that this fellow drives out demons.'
Jesus knew their thoughts and said to them. . .
'If Satan drives out Satan,
he is divided against himself.
How then can his kingdom stand?
But if I drive out demons by the Spirit of God,
then the kingdom of God has come upon you.
And so I tell you,
every sin and blasphemy will be forgiven men,
but the blasphemy against the Spirit
will not be forgiven.'   MATTHEW 12:22,24,25,26,28,31

Woe to those who call evil good and good evil,
who put darkness for light and light for darkness,
who put bitter for sweet and sweet for bitter.
Woe to those who are wise in their own eyes
and clever in their own sight.   ISAIAH 5:20,21

Clothed with Christ

Jesus spoke to them again in parables, saying
'The kingdom of heaven is like a king
who prepared a wedding banquet for his son.
When the king came in to see the guests,
he noticed a man there
who was not wearing wedding clothes.
"Friend," he asked,
"how did you get in here without wedding clothes?"
The man was speechless.
Then the king told the attendants,
"Tie him hand and foot, and throw him outside,
      into the darkness,
where there will be weeping and gnashing of teeth."
For many are invited, but few are chosen.'

MATTHEW 22:1,2,11–14

The Scripture declares
that the whole world is a prisoner of sin,
so that what was promised,
being given through faith in Jesus Christ,
might be given to those who believe.
You are all sons of God through faith in Jesus Christ,
for all of you who were baptised into Christ
have been clothed with Christ.   GALATIANS 3:22,26,27

Dedication of mind, heart and life

Above all else, guard your heart,
for it is the wellspring of life.
Put away perversity from your mouth;
keep corrupt talk far from your lips.
Let your eyes look straight ahead,
fix your gaze directly before you.
Make level paths for your feet
and take only ways that are firm.
Do not swerve to the right or the left;
keep your foot from evil.   PROVERBS 4:23–27

Create in me a pure heart, O God,
and renew a steadfast spirit within me.
Do not cast me from your presence
or take your Holy Spirit from me.
Restore to me the joy of your salvation
and grant me a willing spirit, to sustain me.   PSALM 51:10–12

Do not conform any longer
to the pattern of this world,
but be transformed by the renewing of your mind.
Then you will be able
to test and approve what God's will is –
his good, pleasing and perfect will.
For by the grace given me
I say to every one of you:
Do not think of yourself more highly than you ought,
but rather think of yourself with sober judgement,
in accordance with the measure of faith
God has given you.   ROMANS 12:2,3

Thinking about good things

Again Jesus called the crowd to him and said,
'Listen to me, everyone, and understand this.
Nothing outside a man
can make him "unclean" by going into him.
Rather, it is what comes out of a man
that makes him "unclean".'
After he had left the crowd and entered the house,
his disciples asked him about this parable.
'Are you so dull?' he asked.
'Don't you see that nothing that enters a man
        from the outside
can make him "unclean"?'
He went on,
'What comes out of a man is what makes him "unclean".
For from within, out of men's hearts,
come evil thoughts,
sexual immorality,
theft, murder, adultery,
greed, malice, deceit, lewdness,
envy, slander, arrogance and folly.
All these evils come from inside
and make a man "unclean". '   MARK 7:14–18,20–23

Finally, brothers,
whatever is true, whatever is noble,
whatever is right, whatever is pure,
whatever is lovely, whatever is admirable –
if anything is excellent or praiseworthy –
think about such things.
Whatever you have learned or received
        or heard from me, or seen in me –
put it into practice.
And the God of peace will be with you.   PHILIPPIANS 4:8,9

Holy living

Blessed are they whose ways are blameless,
who walk according to the law of the Lord.
Blessed are they who keep his statutes
and seek him with all their heart.
You have laid down precepts
that are to be fully obeyed.
Oh, that my ways were steadfast
in obeying your decrees!
Then I would not be put to shame
when I consider all your commands.
I will praise you with an upright heart
as I learn your righteous laws.
I will obey your decrees;
do not utterly forsake me.   PSALM 119:1,2,4–8

In a large house
there are articles not only of gold and silver,
but also of wood and clay;
some are for noble purposes and some for ignoble.
If a man cleanses himself from the latter,
he will be an instrument for noble purposes,
made holy, useful to the Master
and prepared to do any good work.
Flee the evil desires of youth,
and pursue righteousness, faith, love and peace,
along with those who call on the Lord
out of a pure heart.   2 TIMOTHY 2:20–22

How can a young man keep his way pure?
By living according to your word.
I seek you with all my heart;
do not let me stray from your commands.
I have hidden your word in my heart
that I might not sin against you.   PSALM 119:9–11

Following instructions

Praise be to you, O Lord;
teach me your decrees.
With my lips I recount all the laws
    that come from your mouth.
I rejoice in following your statutes
as one rejoices in great riches.
I meditate on your precepts
and consider your ways. PSALM 119:12–15

My son, do not forget my teaching,
but keep my commands in your heart,
for they will prolong your life many years
and bring you prosperity.
Let love and faithfulness never leave you;
bind them around your neck,
write them on the tablet of your heart.
Then you will win favour and a good name
in the sight of God and man. PROVERBS 3:1–4

But as for you,
continue in what you have learned
    and have become convinced of,
because you know those from whom you learned it,
and how from infancy you have known
    the holy Scriptures,
which are able to make you wise for salvation
    through faith in Christ Jesus.
All Scripture is God-breathed
and is useful for teaching, rebuking, correcting
and training in righteousness,
so that the man of God may be thoroughly equipped
    for every good work. 2 TIMOTHY 3:14–17

Learning right priorities

'Now, O Lord my God,
you have made your servant king
in place of my father David.
So give your servant
    a discerning heart to govern your people
and to distinguish between right and wrong.
For who is able to govern this great people of yours?'
The Lord was pleased that Solomon had asked for this.
So God said to him,
'Since you have asked for this
and not for long life or wealth for yourself,
nor have asked for the death of your enemies
but for discernment in administering justice,
I will do what you have asked.
I will give you a wise and discerning heart,
so that there will never have been anyone like you,
nor will there ever be.
Moreover, I will give you what you have not asked for –
both riches and honour –
so that in your lifetime
you will have no equal among kings.
And if you walk in my ways
and obey my statutes and commands
as David your father did,
I will give you a long life.'   1 KINGS 3:7,9–14

So do not worry, saying, 'What shall we eat?'
or 'What shall we drink?'
or 'What shall we wear?'
For the pagans run after all these things,
and your heavenly Father knows that you need them.
But seek first his kingdom and his righteousness,
and all these things will be given to you as well.
                                        MATTHEW 6:31–33

To be avoided – pride

This is what the Lord says:
'Let not the wise man boast of his wisdom
or the strong man boast of his strength
or the rich man boast of his riches,
but let him who boasts boast about this:
that he understands and knows me,
that I am the Lord, who exercises kindness,
justice and righteousness on earth,
for in these I delight,'
declares the Lord.   JEREMIAH 9:23,24

May I never boast
except in the cross of our Lord Jesus Christ,
through which the world has been crucified to me,
and I to the world.   GALATIANS 6:14

If anyone else thinks he has reasons
        to put confidence in the flesh,
I have more:
circumcised on the eighth day,
of the people of Israel, of the tribe of Benjamin,
a Hebrew of Hebrews;
in regard to the law, a Pharisee;
as for zeal, persecuting the church;
as for legalistic righteousness, faultless.
But whatever was to my profit
I now consider loss for the sake of Christ.
What is more, I consider everything a loss
compared to the surpassing greatness
of knowing Christ Jesus my Lord,
for whose sake I have lost all things.
I consider them rubbish,
that I may gain Christ and be found in him.
                                            PHILIPPIANS 3:4–8

To be avoided – self-reliance

When I felt secure, I said,
'I shall never be shaken.'
O Lord, when you favoured me,
you made my mountain stand firm;
but when you hid your face,
I was dismayed.   PSALM 30:6,7

To keep me from becoming conceited. . .
there was given me a thorn in my flesh,
a messenger of Satan, to torment me.
Three times I pleaded with the Lord
to take it away from me.
But he said to me,
'My grace is sufficient for you,
for my power is made perfect in weakness.'
Therefore I will boast all the more gladly
about my weaknesses,
so that Christ's power may rest on me.
                    2 CORINTHIANS 12:7–9

Trust in the Lord with all your heart
and lean not on your own understanding;
in all your ways acknowledge him,
and he will make your paths straight.
Do not be wise in your own eyes;
fear the Lord and shun evil.
This will bring health to your body
and nourishment to your bones.   PROVERBS 3:5–8

To be avoided – careless language

No man can tame the tongue.
It is a restless evil,
full of deadly poison.
With the tongue we praise our Lord and Father,
and with it we curse men,
who have been made in God's likeness.
Out of the same mouth come praise and cursing.
My brothers, this should not be.   JAMES 3:8–10

But now you must rid yourselves
of all such things as these:
anger, rage, malice, slander
and filthy language from your lips.
Do not lie to each other. . .   COLOSSIANS 3:8,9

'Woe to me!' I cried.
'I am ruined!
For I am a man of unclean lips,
and I live among a people of unclean lips,
and my eyes have seen the King,
the Lord Almighty.'
Then one of the seraphs flew to me
with a live coal in his hand,
which he had taken with tongs from the altar.
With it he touched my mouth and said,
'See, this has touched your lips;
your guilt is taken away
and your sin atoned for.'   ISAIAH 6:5–7

To be avoided – making rash vows

Again, you have heard
that it was said to the people long ago,
'Do not break your oath,
but keep the oaths you have made to the Lord.'
But I tell you,
Do not swear at all. . .
Simply let your 'Yes' be 'Yes,'
and your 'No,' 'No';
anything beyond this comes from the evil one.

MATTHEW 5:33,34,37

Jephthah made a vow to the Lord:
'If you give the Ammonites into my hands,
whatever comes out of the door of my house
to meet me when I return in triumph from the Ammonites
will be the Lord's,
and I will sacrifice it as a burnt offering.'
Then Jephthah went over to fight the Ammonites,
and the Lord gave them into his hands.
When Jephthah returned to his home in Mizpah,
who should come out to meet him but his daughter. . .

JUDGES 11:30–32,34

Above all, my brothers,
do not swear –
not by heaven or by earth or by anything else.
Let your 'Yes' be 'Yes',
and your 'No', 'No',
or you will be condemned.

JAMES 5:12

To be avoided – misuse of drink

Who has woe? Who has sorrow?
Who has strife? Who has complaints?
Who has needless bruises? Who has bloodshot eyes?
Those who linger over wine,
who go to sample bowls of mixed wine.
Do not gaze at wine when it is red,
when it sparkles in the cup,
when it goes down smoothly!
In the end it bites like a snake
and poisons like a viper.
Your eyes will see strange sights
and your mind imagine confusing things.
You will be like one sleeping on the high seas,
lying on top of the rigging.
'They hit me,' you will say, 'but I'm not hurt!
They beat me, but I don't feel it!
When will I wake up
so I can find another drink?'   PROVERBS 23:29–35

Be very careful, then, how you live –
not as unwise but as wise,
making the most of every opportunity,
because the days are evil.
Therefore do not be foolish,
but understand what the Lord's will is.
Do not get drunk on wine, which leads to debauchery.
Instead, be filled with the Spirit.   EPHESIANS 5:15–18

Woe to those who are heroes at drinking wine
and champions at mixing drinks,
who acquit the guilty for a bribe,
but deny justice to the innocent.   ISAIAH 5:22,23

To be avoided – unfaithfulness

You flood the Lord's altar with tears.
You weep and wail
because he no longer pays attention to your offerings
or accepts them with pleasure from your hands.
You ask, 'Why?'
It is because the Lord is acting as the witness
between you and the wife of your youth,
because you have broken faith with her,
though she is your partner,
the wife of your marriage covenant.
Has not the Lord made them one?
In flesh and spirit they are his. . .
'I hate divorce,' says the Lord God of Israel,
'and I hate a man's covering himself with violence
as well as with his garment,'
says the Lord Almighty.
So guard yourself in your spirit,
and do not break faith.   MALACHI 2:13–15,16

Marriage should be honoured by all,
and the marriage bed kept pure,
for God will judge the adulterer
and all the sexually immoral.   HEBREWS 13:4

At the beginning of creation
God 'made them male and female.'
'For this reason a man will leave his father and mother
and be united to his wife,
and the two will become one flesh.'
So they are no longer two, but one.
Therefore what God has joined together,
let man not separate.   MARK 10:6–9

To be avoided – dependence on wealth

This is what the Lord says:
'Let not the wise man boast of his wisdom
or the strong man boast of his strength
or the rich man boast of his riches. . . '   JEREMIAH 9:23

Remember the Lord your God,
for it is he who gives you the ability
      to produce wealth,
and so confirms his covenant,
which he swore to your forefathers,
as it is today.
If you ever forget the Lord your God
and follow other gods
and worship and bow down to them,
I testify against you today
that you will surely be destroyed.   DEUTERONOMY 8:18,19

No-one can serve two masters.
Either he will hate the one and love the other,
or he will be devoted to the one and despise the other.
You cannot serve both God and Money.
Therefore I tell you,
do not worry about your life,
what you will eat or drink;
or about your body,
what you will wear.
Is not life more important than food,
and the body more important than clothes?
Look at the birds of the air;
they do not sow or reap or store away in barns,
and yet your heavenly Father feeds them.
Are you not much more valuable than they?
                              MATTHEW 6:24–26

To be avoided – the love of riches

Keep your lives free from the love of money
and be content with what you have,
because God has said,
'Never will I leave you;
never will I forsake you.'   HEBREWS 13:5

Whoever loves money never has money enough;
whoever loves wealth
is never satisfied with his income.
This too is meaningless.
The sleep of a labourer is sweet,
whether he eats little or much,
but the abundance of a rich man
permits him no sleep.
I have seen a grievous evil under the sun:
wealth hoarded to the harm of its owner,
or wealth lost through some misfortune,
so that when he has a son
there is nothing left for him.
Naked a man comes from his mother's womb,
and as he comes, so he departs.
He takes nothing from his labour
that he can carry in his hand.   ECCLESIASTES 5:10,12–15

Do not be owerawed when a man grows rich,
when the splendour of his house increases;
for he will take nothing with him when he dies,
his splendour will not descend with him.
A man who has riches without understanding
is like the beasts that perish.   PSALM 49:16,17,20

To be avoided – luxurious living

Your wealth has rotted,
and moths have eaten your clothes.
Your gold and silver are corroded.
Their corrosion will testify against you
and eat your flesh like fire.
You have hoarded wealth in the last days.
You have lived on earth in luxury and self-indulgence.
You have fattened yourselves in the day of slaughter.

JAMES 5:2,3,5

Do not store up for yourselves treasures on earth,
where moth and rust destroy,
and where thieves break in and steal.
But store up for yourselves treasures in heaven,
where moth and rust do not destroy,
and where thieves do not break in and steal.
For where your treasure is,
there your heart will be also.   MATTHEW 6:19–21

He has given us new birth into a living hope
through the resurrection of Jesus Christ from the dead,
and into an inheritance
that can never perish, spoil or fade –
kept in heaven for you,
who through faith are shielded by God's power
until the coming of the salvation
that is ready to be revealed in the last time.   1 PETER 1:3–5

To be avoided – envy

Do not envy wicked men,
do not desire their company;
for their hearts plot violence,
and their lips talk about making trouble.   PROVERBS 24:1,2

But as for me, my feet had almost slipped;
I had nearly lost my foothold.
For I envied the arrogant
when I saw the prosperity of the wicked.
When I tried to understand all this,
it was oppressive to me
till I entered the sanctuary of God;
then I understood their final destiny.
Surely you place them on slippery ground;
you cast them down to ruin.
How suddenly are they destroyed,
completely swept away by terrors!
As a dream when one awakes,
so when you arise, O Lord,
you will despise them as fantasies.
Those who are far from you will perish;
you destroy all who are unfaithful to you.
But as for me, it is good to be near God.
I have made the Sovereign Lord my refuge;
I will tell of all your deeds.   PSALM 73:2,3,16–20,27,28

To be avoided – complacency

Jesus told them this parable:
'The ground of a certain rich man produced a good crop.
He thought to himself,
"What shall I do? I have no place to store my crops."
Then he said, "This is what I'll do.
I will tear down my barns and build bigger ones,
and there I will store all my grain and my goods.
And I'll say to myself,
'You have plenty of good things
laid up for many years.
Take life easy;
eat, drink and be merry.' "
But God said to him, "You fool!
This very night your life will be demanded from you.
Then who will get what you have prepared
for yourself?"
This is how it will be
with anyone who stores up things for himself
but is not rich towards God.'   LUKE 12:16–21

Do not boast about tomorrow,
for you do not know
what a day may bring forth.   PROVERBS 27:1

To be avoided – unforgiveness

Do not repay anyone evil for evil.
Be careful to do what is right
    in the eyes of everybody.
If it is possible,
as far as it depends on you,
live at peace with everyone.
Do not take revenge, my friends,
but leave room for God's wrath,
for it is written:
'It is mine to avenge: I will repay,'
says the Lord.
On the contrary:
'If your enemy is hungry, feed him;
if he is thirsty, give him something to drink.
In doing this, you will heap burning coals
on his head.'
Do not be overcome by evil;
but overcome evil with good.   ROMANS 12:17–21

When they came to the place called The Skull,
there they crucified him,
along with the criminals –
one on his right, the other on his left.
Jesus said,
'Father, forgive them,
for they do not know what they are doing.'   LUKE 23:33,34

To be avoided – revenge

You have heard that it was said,
'Eye for eye, and tooth for tooth.'
But I tell you,
Do not resist an evil person.
If someone strikes you on the right cheek,
turn to him the other also.
And if someone wants to sue you
and take your tunic,
let him have your cloak as well.
If someone forces you to go one mile,
go with him two miles.
Give to the one who asks you,
and do not turn away from the one
who wants to borrow from you.   MATTHEW 5:38–42

Do not repay evil with evil
or insult with insult,
but with blessing,
because to this you were called
so that you may inherit a blessing.
For, 'Whoever would love life and see good days
must keep his tongue from evil
and his lips from deceitful speech.
He must turn from evil and do good;
he must seek peace and pursue it.'   1 PETER 3:9–11

To be avoided – spiritism and the occult

Do not turn to mediums
or seek out spiritists,
for you will be defiled by them.
I am the Lord your God.   LEVITICUS 19:31

So Saul disguised himself, putting on other clothes,
and at night he and two men went to the woman.
'Consult a spirit for me,' he said,
'and bring up for me the one I name.'
Then the woman asked,
'Whom shall I bring up for you?'
'Bring up Samuel,' he said.
The woman said,
'I see a spirit coming up out of the ground.'
'What does he look like?' he asked.
'An old man wearing a robe is coming up,' she said.
Then Saul knew it was Samuel. . .
Samuel said. . .
'The Lord will hand over both Israel and you
to the Philistines,
and tomorrow you and your sons will be with me.
The Lord will also hand over
the army of Israel to the Philistines.'
Immediately Saul fell full length on the ground,
filled with fear because of Samuel's words. . .
       1 SAMUEL 28:8,11,13,14,19,20

The idols speak deceit.
Diviners see visions that lie,
they tell dreams that are false.
They give comfort in vain.
Therefore the people wander like sheep
oppressed for lack of a shepherd.   ZECHARIAH 10:2

To be avoided – spiritism and the occult

When men tell you to consult mediums and spiritists,
who whisper and mutter,
should not a people enquire of their God?
Why consult the dead on behalf of the living?
To the law and to the testimony!
If they do not speak according to this word,
they have no light of dawn.   ISAIAH 8:19,20

When you enter the land
the Lord your God is giving you,
do not learn to imitate
the detestable ways of the nations there.
Let no-one be found among you
who sacrifices his son or daughter in the fire,
who practises divination or sorcery,
interprets omens, engages in witchcraft,
or casts spells,
or who is a medium or spiritist
or who consults the dead.
Anyone who does these things is detestable to the Lord,
and because of these detestable practices
the Lord your God will drive out
        those nations before you.
You must be blameless before the Lord your God.
The nations you will dispossess
listen to those who practise sorcery or divination.
But as for you,
the Lord your God has not permitted you to do so.
                              DEUTERONOMY 18:9–14

Avoiding spiritual compromise

Ephraim mixes with the nations;
Ephraim is a flat cake not turned over.
Foreigners sap his strength,
but he does not realise it.
His hair is sprinkled with grey,
but he does not notice.
Ephraim is like a dove,
easily deceived and senseless –
now calling to Egypt, now turning to Assyria.
When they go, I will throw my net over them;
I will pull them down like birds of the air.
When I hear them flocking together,
I will catch them.
Woe to them,
because they have strayed from me!
Destruction to them,
because they have rebelled against me!
I long to redeem them
but they speak lies against me. · · · · · HOSEA 7:8,9,11–13

Do not be yoked together with unbelievers.
For what do righteousness and wickedness
       have in common?
Or what fellowship can light have with darkness?
What harmony is there between Christ and Belial?
What does a believer have in common
       with an unbeliever?
What agreement is there
       between the temple of God and idols?
For we are the temple of the living God. . .
· · · · · · · · · · · 2 CORINTHIANS 6:14–16

Expect God's testing

As a man disciplines his son,
so the Lord your God disciplines you.
Observe the commands of the Lord your God,
walking in his ways and revering him.   DEUTERONOMY 8:5,6

Those whom I love I rebuke and discipline.
So be earnest, and repent.
To him who overcomes,
I will give the right to sit with me
     on my throne,
just as I overcame and sat down with my Father
on his throne.   REVELATION 3:19,21

The Lord is compassionate and gracious,
slow to anger, abounding in love.
He will not always accuse,
nor will he harbour his anger for ever;
he does not treat us as our sins deserve
or repay us according to our iniquities.
For as high as the heavens are above the earth,
so great is his love for those who fear him;
as far as the east is from the west,
so far has he removed our transgressions from us.
As a father has compassion on his children,
so the Lord has compassion on those who fear him;
for he knows how we are formed,
he remembers that we are dust.   PSALM 103:8–14

Welcome God's discipline

Blessed is the man whom God corrects;
so do not despise the discipline of the Almighty.
For he wounds, but he also binds up;
he injures, but his hands also heal.   JOB 5:17,18

My son, do not despise the Lord's discipline
and do not resent his rebuke,
because the Lord disciplines those he loves,
as a father the son he delights in.   PROVERBS 3:11,12

Endure hardship as discipline;
God is treating you as sons.
For what son is not disciplined by his father?
If you are not disciplined
(and everyone undergoes discipline),
then you are illegitimate children
     and not true sons.
Moreover,
we have all had human fathers who disciplined us
and we respected them for it.
How much more should we submit
     to the Father of our spirits and live!
Our fathers disciplined us for a little while
     as they thought best;
but God disciplines us for our good,
that we may share in his holiness.
No discipline seems pleasant at the time, but painful.
Later on, however,
it produces a harvest of righteousness and peace
for those who have been trained by it.   HEBREWS 12:7–11

Accept God's correction

A voice came down from heaven,
'This is what is decreed for you, King Nebuchadnezzar:
Your royal authority has been taken from you.
You will be driven away from people
and will live with the wild animals;
you will eat grass like cattle.
Seven times will pass by for you
until you acknowledge
that the Most High is sovereign
over the kingdoms of men
and gives them to anyone he wishes.'
Immediately
what had been said about Nebuchadnezzar
was fulfilled. . .
At the end of that time,
I, Nebuchadnezzar,
raised my eyes towards heaven,
and my sanity was restored.
Then I praised the Most High;
I honoured and glorified him who lives for ever.

DANIEL 4:31–33,34

Do good to your servant
according to your word, O Lord.
Teach me knowledge and good judgement,
for I believe in your commands.
Before I was afflicted I went astray,
but now I obey your word.
You are good, and what you do is good;
teach me your decrees.
It was good for me to be afflicted
so that I might learn your decrees.

PSALM 119:65–68,71

Persistent living

Then the Lord rained down burning sulphur
on Sodom and Gomorrah –
from the Lord out of the heavens.
Thus he overthrew those cities and the entire plain,
including all those living in the cities –
and also the vegetation in the land.
But Lot's wife looked back
and she became a pillar of salt.   GENESIS 19:24–26

Another man said,
'I will follow you, Lord;
but first let me go back
and say good-bye to my family.'
Jesus replied,
'No-one who puts his hand to the plough and looks back
is fit for service in the kingdom of God.'   LUKE 9:61,62

Demas,
because he loved this world,
has deserted me and has gone to Thessalonica.
Crescens has gone to Galatia,
and Titus to Dalmatia.
Only Luke is with me. . .   2 TIMOTHY 4:9–11

We want each of you to show
        this same diligence to the very end,
in order to make your hope sure.
We do not want you to become lazy,
but to imitate those who through faith and patience
        inherit what has been promised.   HEBREWS 6:11,12

Self-sacrifice

When they had finished eating,
Jesus said to Simon Peter. . .
'I tell you the truth,
when you were younger
you dressed yourself and went where you wanted;
but when you are old you will stretch out your hands,
and someone else will dress you and lead you
        where you do not want to go.'
Jesus said this to indicate the kind of death
by which Peter would glorify God.
Then he said to him, 'Follow me!'   JOHN 21:15,18,19

Then Jesus called the crowd to him
        along with his disciples
and said:
'If anyone would come after me,
he must deny himself
and take up his cross and follow me.
For whoever wants to save his life will lose it,
but whoever loses his life for me and for the gospel
        will save it.
What good is it for a man to gain the whole world,
yet forfeit his soul?
Or what can a man give in exchange for his soul?'

MARK 8:34–37

The need for faith

Thomas declared,
'Unless I see the nail marks in his hands
and put my finger where the nails were,
and put my hand into his side,
I will not believe it.'
A week later his disciples were in the house again,
and Thomas was with them.
Though the doors were locked,
Jesus came and stood among them,
and said, 'Peace be with you!'
Then he said to Thomas,
'Put your finger here; see my hands.
Reach out your hand and put it into my side.
Stop doubting and believe.'
Thomas answered, 'My Lord and my God!'
Then Jesus told him,
'Because you have seen me, you have believed;
blessed are those who have not seen
and yet have believed.'   JOHN 20:25–29

Israel served the Lord
throughout the lifetime of Joshua
and of the elders who outlived him
and who had experienced everything
        the Lord had done for Israel.   JOSHUA 24:31

'Unless you people
        see miraculous signs and wonders,'
Jesus told him,
'you will never believe.'   JOHN 4:48

Do you still have no faith?

Others went out on the sea in ships;
they were merchants on the mighty waters.
They saw the works of the Lord,
his wonderful deeds in the deep.
For he spoke and stirred up a tempest
that lifted high the waves.
They mounted up to the heavens
and went down to the depths. . .
Then they cried out to the Lord in their trouble,
and he brought them out of their distress.
He stilled the storm to a whisper;
the waves of the sea were hushed.   PSALM 107:23–26,28,29

The disciples woke Jesus and said to him,
'Teacher, don't you care if we drown?'
He got up, rebuked the wind and said to the waves,
'Quiet! Be still!'
Then the wind died down and it was completely calm.
He said to his disciples,
'Why are you so afraid?
Do you still have no faith?'   MARK 4:38–40

If any of you lacks wisdom, he should ask God,
who gives generously to all without finding fault;
and it will be given to him.
But when he asks,
he must believe and not doubt,
because he who doubts is like a wave of the sea,
blown and tossed by the wind.
That man should not think he will receive anything
      from the Lord;
he is a double-minded man,
unstable in all he does.   JAMES 1:5–8

What the Lord commands

And now, O Israel,
what does the Lord your God ask of you
but to fear the Lord your God,
to walk in all his ways,
to love him,
to serve the Lord your God with all your heart
and with all your soul,
and to observe the Lord's commands and decrees
that I am giving you today for your own good?
To the Lord your God belong the heavens,
even the highest heavens,
the earth and everything in it.
Yet the Lord set his affection on your forefathers
    and loved them,
and he chose you, their descendants,
above all the nations, as it is today.
Circumcise your hearts, therefore,
and do not be stiff-necked any longer.

DEUTERONOMY 10:12–16

As obedient children,
do not conform to the evil desires you had
    when you lived in ignorance.
But just as he who called you is holy,
so be holy in all you do;
for it is written,
'Be holy, because I am holy.'   1 PETER 1:14–16

Fear the Lord your God and serve him.
Hold fast to him
and take your oaths in his name.
He is your praise; he is your God. . .

DEUTERONOMY 10:20,21

Growing out of immaturity

Brothers,
I could not address you as spiritual
but as wordly –
mere infants in Christ.
I gave you milk, not solid food,
for you were not yet ready for it.
Indeed, you are still not ready.
You are still wordly.
For since there is jealousy and quarrelling among you,
are you not worldly?
Are you not acting like mere men?   1 CORINTHIANS 3:1–3

Though by this time you ought to be teachers,
you need someone to teach you the elementary truths of
    God's word all over again.
You need milk, not solid food!
Anyone who lives on milk,
being still an infant,
is not acquainted with the teaching about righteousness.
But solid food is for the mature,
who by constant use have trained themselves
to distinguish good from evil.
Therefore let us leave
the elementary teachings about Christ
and go on to maturity. . .   HEBREWS 5:12–6:1

Sound foundation, careful building

Everyone who hears these words of mine
and puts them into practice
is like a wise man who built his house on the rock.
The rain came down, the streams rose,
and the winds blew and beat against that house;
yet it did not fall,
because it had its foundation on the rock.
But everyone who hears these words of mine
and does not put them into practice
is like a foolish man who built his house on sand.
The rain came down, the streams rose,
and the winds blew and beat against that house,
and it fell with a great crash.   MATTHEW 7:24–27

We are God's fellow-workers;
you are God's field, God's building.
By the grace God has given me,
I laid a foundation as an expert builder,
and someone else is building on it.
But each one should be careful how he builds.
For no-one can lay any foundation
other than the one already laid,
which is Jesus Christ.
If any man builds on this foundation
using gold, silver, costly stones,
wood, hay or straw,
his work will be shown for what it is,
because the Day will bring it to light.
It will be revealed with fire,
and the fire will test the quality
of each man's work.   1 CORINTHIANS 3:9–13

Increasing dependence on Christ

Fruit trees of all kinds
will grow on both banks of the river.
Their leaves will not wither,
nor will their fruit fail.
Every month they will bear,
because the water from the sanctuary flows to them.
Their fruit will serve for food
and their leaves for healing.   EZEKIEL 47:12

I am the true vine
and my Father is the gardener.
He cuts off every branch in me
that bears no fruit,
while every branch that does bear fruit
he trims clean so that it will be even more fruitful.
Remain in me, and I will remain in you.
No branch can bear fruit by itself;
it must remain in the vine.
Neither can you bear fruit
unless you remain in me.
I am the vine; you are the branches.
If a man remains in me and I in him,
he will bear much fruit;
apart from me you can do nothing.
If you remain in me and my words remain in you,
ask whatever you wish, and it will be given you.
This is to my Father's glory,
that you bear much fruit,
showing yourselves to be my disciples.
You did not choose me,
but I chose you to go and bear fruit –
fruit that will last. . .   JOHN 15:1,2,4,5,7,8,16

Conscious effort

Make every effort to add to your faith goodness;
and to goodness, knowledge;
and to knowledge, self-control;
and to self-control, perseverance;
and to perseverance, godliness;
and to godliness, brotherly kindness;
and to brotherly kindness, love.
For if you possess these qualities
      in increasing measure,
they will keep you from being ineffective
and unproductive in your knowledge of our Lord Jesus
      Christ.
Therefore, my brothers, be all the more eager
to make your calling and election sure.
For if you do these things, you will never fall,
and you will receive a rich welcome
into the eternal kingdom of our Lord and Saviour
Jesus Christ.　　　　　　　　　　　2 PETER 1:5–8,10,11

But you, dear friends,
build yourselves up in your most holy faith
and pray in the Holy Spirit.
Keep yourselves in God's love
as you wait for the mercy of our Lord Jesus Christ
      to bring you to eternal life.　　　　　JUDE 20,21

And this is my prayer:
that your love may abound more and more
in knowledge and depth of insight,
so that you may be able to discern what is best
and may be pure and blameless until the day of Christ.
　　　　　　　　　　　　　　　　PHILIPPIANS 1:9,10

Strengthening faith

This is the victory that has overcome the world,
even our faith.
Who is it that overcomes the world?
Only he who believes
      that Jesus is the Son of God.   1 JOHN 5:4,5

Now faith is being sure of what we hope for
and certain of what we do not see.   HEBREWS 11:1

The apostles said to the Lord,
'Increase our faith!'
He replied,
'If you have faith as small as a mustard seed,
  you can say to this mulberry tree,
"Be uprooted and planted in the sea,"
and it will obey you.'   LUKE 17:5,6

So then,
just as you received Christ Jesus as Lord,
continue to live in him,
rooted and built up in him,
strengthened in the faith as you were taught,
and overflowing with thankfulness.   COLOSSIANS 2:6,7

The source of strength and endurance

I pray also
that the eyes of your heart may be enlightened
in order that you may know
the hope to which he has called you,
the riches of his glorious inheritance in the saints,
and his incomparably great power for us who believe.
That power is like the working of his mighty strength,
which he exerted in Christ
when he raised him from the dead
and seated him at his right hand
    in the heavenly realms.   EPHESIANS 1:18–20

Do not let your hands hang limp.
The Lord your God is with you,
he is mighty to save.
He will take great delight in you,
he will quiet you with his love,
he will rejoice over you with singing.   ZEPHANIAH 3:16,17

He will keep you strong to the end,
so that you will be blameless
on the day of our Lord Jesus Christ.
God, who has called you
into fellowship with his Son Jesus Christ our Lord,
    is faithful.   1 CORINTHIANS 1:8,9

To him who is able to keep you from falling
and to present you before his glorious presence
without fault and with great joy –
to the only God our Saviour
be glory, majesty, power and authority,
through Jesus Christ our Lord,
before all ages, now and for evermore! Amen.   JUDE 24,25

The goal of Christian growth

I kneel before the Father,
from whom the whole family in heaven and on earth
    derives its name.
I pray that out of his glorious riches
he may strengthen you with power
through his Spirit in your inner being,
so that Christ may dwell in your hearts
    through faith.
And I pray that you,
being rooted and established in love,
may have power, together with all the saints,
to grasp how wide and long and high and deep
    is the love of Christ,
and to know this love that surpasses knowledge –
that you may be filled to the measure
of all the fullness of God.   EPHESIANS 3:14–19

It was he who gave some to be apostles,
some to be prophets, some to be evangelists,
and some to be pastors and teachers,
to prepare God's people for works of service,
so that the body of Christ may be built up
until we all reach unity in the faith
and in the knowledge of the Son of God
and become mature,
attaining to the whole measure
of the fullness of Christ.
Then we will no longer be infants. . .
Instead, speaking the truth in love,
we will in all things
grow up into him who is the Head,
that is, Christ.   EPHESIANS 4:11–14,15

The vision of God

Taking one of the stones there,
Jacob put it under his head and lay down to sleep.
He had a dream in which he saw
　　a stairway resting on the earth,
with its top reaching to heaven,
and the angels of God
were ascending and descending on it.
There above it stood the Lord, and he said:
'I am with you
and will watch over you wherever you go,
and I will bring you back to this land.
I will not leave you
　　until I have done what I have promised you.'
When Jacob awoke from his sleep, he thought,
'Surely the Lord is in this place,
and I was not aware of it.'
He was afraid and said,
'How awesome is this place!
This is none other than the house of God;
this is the gate of heaven.'　　　　　GENESIS 28:11–13,15–17

Jesus said. . .
'I tell you the truth,
you shall see heaven open,
and the angels of God ascending and descending
　　on the Son of Man.'　　　　　　　　JOHN 1:50,51

Stephen, full of the Holy Spirit,
looked up to heaven and saw the glory of God,
and Jesus standing at the right hand of God,
'Look,' he said, 'I see heaven open
and the Son of Man
　　standing at the right hand of God.'　　ACTS 7:55,56

Spiritual simplicity

My heart is not proud, O Lord,
my eyes are not haughty;
I do not concern myself with great matters
or things too wonderful for me.
But I have stilled and quieted my soul;
like a weaned child with its mother,
like a weaned child is my soul within me.   PSALM 131:1,2

Make my joy complete by being like-minded,
having the same love,
being one in spirit and purpose.
Do nothing out of selfish ambition or vain conceit,
but in humility consider others better than yourselves.
Each of you should look not only to your own interests,
but also to the interests of others.   PHILIPPIANS 2:2–4

Come to me,
all you who are weary and burdened,
and I will give you rest.
Take my yoke upon you and learn from me,
for I am gentle and humble in heart,
and you will find rest for your souls.
For my yoke is easy
and my burden is light.   MATTHEW 11:28–30

Humility before men

Do not exalt yourself in the king's presence,
and do not claim a place among great men;
it is better for him to say to you, 'Come up here,'
than for him to humiliate you before a nobleman.

PROVERBS 25:6,7

Then the chief cupbearer said to Pharaoh. . .
'A young Hebrew was there with us,
a servant of the captain of the guard.
We told him our dreams,
and he interpreted them for us,
giving each man the interpretation of his dream.'
So Pharaoh sent for Joseph,
and he was quickly brought from the dungeon. . .
Joseph's plan seemed good to Pharaoh
and to all his officials.
So Pharaoh asked them,
'Can we find anyone like this man,
one in whom is the spirit of God?'
Then Pharaoh said to Joseph,
'Since God has made all this known to you,
there is no-one so discerning and wise as you.
You shall be in charge of my palace,
and all my people are to submit to your orders.
Only with respect to the throne
    will I be greater than you.'   GENESIS 41:9,12,14,37–39

The Lord brings death and makes alive;
he brings down to the grave and raises up.
The Lord sends poverty and wealth;
he humbles and he exalts.
He raises the poor from the dust
and lifts the needy from the ash heap;
he seats them with princes
and has them inherit a throne of honour. . .   1 SAMUEL 2:6–8

The servant

At that time
the disciples came to Jesus and asked,
'Who is the greatest in the kingdom of heaven?'
He called a little child
and had him stand among them.
And he said:
'I tell you the truth, unless you change
and become like little children,
you will never enter the kingdom of heaven.
Therefore, whoever humbles himself like this child
is the greatest in the kingdom of heaven.'

MATTHEW 18:1–4

Whoever wants to become great among you
must be your servant,
and whoever wants to be first
must be slave of all.
For even the Son of Man
did not come to be served, but to serve,
and to give his life as a ransom for many.   MARK 10:43–45

Christ Jesus, being in very nature God,
did not consider equality with God
        something to be grasped,
but made himself nothing,
taking the very nature of a servant,
being made in human likeness.
And being found in appearance as a man,
he humbled himself
and became obedient to death –
even death on a cross!   PHILIPPIANS 2:6–8

Christ-like humility

Your attitude should be the same
      as that of Christ Jesus:
Who made himself nothing,
taking the very nature of a servant,
being made in human likeness.   PHILIPPIANS 2:5,7

Jesus got up from the meal,
took off his outer clothing,
and wrapped a towel round his waist.
After that, he poured water into a basin
and began to wash his disciples' feet,
drying them with the towel
      that was wrapped around him.
When he had finished washing their feet,
he put on his clothes
and returned to his place.
'Do you understand what I have done for you?'
he asked them.
'You call me "Teacher" and "Lord",
and rightly so, for that is what I am.
Now that I, your Lord and Teacher,
have washed your feet,
you also should wash one another's feet.
I have set you an example
that you should do as I have done for you.'
      JOHN 13:4,5,12–15

Clothe yourselves with humility towards one another,
because, 'God opposes the proud
but gives grace to the humble.'
Humble yourselves, therefore, under God's mighty hand,
that he may lift you up in due time.   1 PETER 5:5,6

The child

A young girl from Israel . . . served Naaman's wife.
She said to her mistress,
'If only my master would see the prophet
    who is in Samaria!
He would cure him of his leprosy.'
Naaman went to his master
and told him what the girl from Israel had said.

2 KINGS 5:2–4

'Where shall we buy bread
for these people to eat?'
Philip answered him,
'Eight months' wages
would not buy enough bread
for each one to have a bite!'
Another of his disciples,
Andrew, Simon Peter's brother, spoke up,
'Here is a boy with five small barley loaves
and two small fish.'

JOHN 6:5, 7–9

Josiah was eight years old when he became king,
and he reigned in Jerusalem for thirty-one years.
His mother's name was Jedidah daughter of Adaiah;
she was from Bozkath.
He did what was right in the eyes of the Lord
and walked in all the ways of his father David,
not turning aside to the right or to the left.   2 KINGS 22:1, 2

The young person

Light is sweet,
and it pleases the eyes to see the sun.
However many years a man may live,
let him enjoy them all . . .
Be happy, young man, while you are young,
and let your heart give you joy
    in the days of your youth.
Follow the ways of your heart
and whatever your eyes see,
but know that for all these things
God will bring you to judgement.
So then, banish anxiety from your heart
and cast off the troubles of your body. . .
Remember your Creator in the days of your youth,
before the days of trouble come
and the years approach when you will say,
'I find no pleasure in them.'   ECCLESIASTES 11:7-10;12:1

We are consumed by your anger
and terrified by your indignation.
You have set our iniquities before you,
our secret sins in the light of your presence.
All our days pass away under your wrath;
we finish our years with a moan.
The length of our days is seventy years –
or eighty, if we have the strength;
yet their span is but trouble and sorrow,
for they quickly pass, and we fly away.
Who knows the power of your anger?
For your wrath is as great
    as the fear that is due to you.
Teach us to number our days aright,
that we may gain a heart of wisdom.   PSALM 90:7–12

The young person

David asked the men standing near him,
'What will be done for the man
    who kills this Philistine
and removes the disgrace from Israel?'
When Eliab, David's oldest brother,
heard him speaking with the men,
he burned with anger at him and asked,
'Why have you come down here?
And with whom did you leave those few sheep
    in the desert?
I know how conceited you are
and how wicked your heart is;
you came down only to watch the battle.'
'Now what have I done?' said David.
'Can't I even speak?'
What David said was overheard and reported to Saul,
and Saul sent for him.
David said to Saul,
'Let no-one lose heart on account of this Philistine;
your servant will go and fight him.'

1 SAMUEL 17:26,28,29,31,32

This is a trustworthy saying
that deserves full acceptance
(and for this we labour and strive),
that we have put our hope in the living God,
who is the Saviour of all men,
and especially of those who believe.
Command and teach these things.
Don't let anyone look down on you
    because you are young,
but set an example for the believers
in speech, in life, in love, in faith and in purity.

1 TIMOTHY 4:9–12

The man

Cornelius and all his family
were devout and God-fearing;
he gave generously to those in need
and prayed to God regularly.
One day . . . he had a vision.
He distinctly saw an angel of God,
who came to him and said,
'Cornelius!
. . . Your prayers and gifts to the poor
have come up as a remembrance before God.'

ACTS 10:2, 3, 4

The Lord says:
'. . . Blessed is the man who trusts in the Lord,
whose confidence is in him.
He will be like a tree planted by the water
that sends out its roots by the stream.
It does not fear when heat comes.'   JEREMIAH 17:7,8

Even in darkness light dawns for the upright,
for the gracious and compassionate
       and righteous man.
Good will come to him who is generous
and lends freely,
who conducts his affairs with justice.
Surely he will never be shaken;
a righteous man will be remembered for ever.
He will have no fear of bad news;
his heart is steadfast, trusting in the Lord.
His heart is secure, he will have no fear;
in the end he will look in triumph on his foes.
He has scattered abroad his gifts to the poor,
his righteousness endures for ever.   PSALM 112:4–9

The woman

Your beauty
should not come from outward adornment,
such as braided hair
and the wearing of gold jewellery
      and fine clothes.
Instead,
it should be that of your inner self,
the unfading beauty of a gentle and quiet spirit,
which is of great worth in God's sight.
For this is the way the holy women of the past
who put their hope in God
used to make themselves beautiful.
They were submissive to their own husbands,
like Sarah,
who obeyed Abraham and called him her master.
You are her daughters if you do what is right
and do not give way to fear.   1 PETER 3:3–6

Mary sat at the Lord's feet
listening to what he said . . .
Martha came to Jesus and asked,
'Lord, don't you care
that my sister has left me to do
      the work by myself?
Tell her to help me!'
'Martha, Martha,' the Lord answered,
'you are worried and upset about many things,
but only one thing is needed.
Mary has chosen what is better,
and it will not be taken away from her.'   LUKE 10:39,40,41,42

The woman

One of those listening was a woman named Lydia,
a dealer in purple cloth from the city of Thyatira,
who was a worshipper of God.
The Lord opened her heart
to respond to Paul's message.
When she and the members of her household were
      baptised,
she invited us to her home.
'If you consider me a believer in the Lord,'
      she said,
'come and stay at my house.'   ACTS 16:14,15

As Hannah kept on praying to the Lord,
Eli observed her mouth.
Hannah was praying in her heart,
and her lips were moving
but her voice was not heard.
Eli thought she was drunk.
'Not so, my lord,' Hannah replied,
'I am a woman who is deeply troubled.
I have not been drinking wine or beer;
I was pouring out my soul to the Lord.'
Eli answered, 'Go in peace,
and may the God of Israel
      grant you what you have asked of him.'
She said,
'May your servant find favour in your eyes.'
                           1 SAMUEL 1:12,13,15,17,18

The woman said to her husband,
'I know that this man who often comes our way
      is a holy man of God.
Let's make a small room on the roof
and put in it a bed and a table,
      a chair and a lamp for him.
Then he can stay there whenever he comes to us.'
                           2 KINGS 4:9,10

Courtship

The Lord God said,
'It is not good for the man to be alone.
I will make a helper suitable for him.'
He caused the man to fall into a deep sleep;
and while he was sleeping,
he took one of the man's ribs
and closed up the place with flesh.
Then the Lord God made a woman from the rib,
and he brought her to the man.
The man said,
'This is now bone of my bones
and flesh of my flesh;
she shall be called "woman",
for she was taken out of man.'   GENESIS 2:18,21–23

My lover spoke and said to me,
'Arise, my darling, my beautiful one,
and come with me.
See! The winter is past, the rains are over and gone.
Flowers appear on the earth;
the season of singing has come,
the cooing of doves is heard in our land.
The fig-tree forms its early fruit;
the blossoming vines spread their fragrance.
Arise, come, my darling;
my beautiful one, come with me.'
'My dove in the clefts of the rock,
in the hiding-places on the mountainside,
show me your face, let me hear your voice. . .
How beautiful you are, my darling!
Oh, how beautiful!
Your eyes are doves.'   SONG OF SONGS 2:10–14;1:15

The betrothal

Before he had finished praying,
Rebekah came out with her jar on her shoulder.
She was the daughter of Bethuel son of Milcah,
who was the wife of Abraham's brother Nahor.
The girl was very beautiful, a virgin. . .   GENESIS 24:15,16

How beautiful you are, my darling!
Oh, how beautiful!
Your eyes behind your veil are doves.
Your hair is like a flock of goats
descending from Mount Gilead.
All beautiful you are, my darling;
there is no flaw in you.
Come with me from Lebanon, my bride,
come with me from Lebanon.
Descend from the crest of Amana,
from the top of Senir, the summit of Hermon,
from the lions' dens
and the mountain haunts of the leopards.
You have stolen my heart, my sister, my bride;
you have stolen my heart with one glance of your eyes,
with one jewel of your necklace.
How delightful is your love, my sister, my bride!
How much more pleasing is your love than wine,
and the fragrance of your perfume than any spice!
Your lips drop sweetness as the honeycomb, my bride;
milk and honey are under your tongue.
The fragrance of your garments
        is like that of Lebanon.   SONG OF SONGS 4:1,7–11

Isaac brought Rebekah
into the tent of his mother Sarah,
and he married Rebekah.
So she became his wife, and he loved her;
and Isaac was comforted after his mother's death.

                                              GENESIS 24:67

Faithfulness

Marriage should be honoured by all,
and the marriage bed kept pure,
for God will judge the adulterer
    and all the sexually immoral.   HEBREWS 13:4

Then Nathan said to David, 'You are the man!
This is what the Lord, the God of Israel, says:
"I anointed you king over Israel. . .
And if all this had been too little,
I would have given you even more.
Why did you despise the word of the Lord
by doing what is evil in his eyes?
You struck down Uriah the Hittite with the sword
and took his wife to be your own . . .
Out of your own household
I am going to bring calamity upon you." '
Then David said to Nathan,
'I have sinned against the Lord.'
Nathan replied, 'The Lord has taken away your sin.
You are not going to die.'   2 SAMUEL 12:7,8,9,11,13

Drink water from your own cistern,
running water from your own well.
Should your springs overflow in the streets,
your streams of water in the public squares?
Let them be yours alone,
never to be shared with strangers.
May your fountain be blessed,
and may you rejoice in the wife of your youth. . .
May you ever be captivated by her love.
    PROVERBS 5:15–18,19

The husband

Husbands, love your wives,
just as Christ loved the church
and gave himself up for her.
Husbands ought to love their wives
    as their own bodies.
He who loves his wife loves himself.
After all, no-one ever hated his own body,
but he feeds and cares for it,
just as Christ does the church –
for we are members of his body.
'For this reason a man will leave his father and mother
and be united to his wife,
and the two will become one flesh.'
Each one of you also must love his wife
    as he loves himself,
and the wife must respect her husband.

EPHESIANS 5:25,28–31,33

Blessed are all who fear the Lord,
who walk in his ways.
You will eat the fruit of your labour;
blessings and prosperity will be yours.
Your wife will be like a fruitful vine
    within your house;
your sons will be like olive shoots
    round your table.
Thus is the man blessed who fears the Lord.
May the Lord bless you from Zion
all the days of your life;
may you see the prosperity of Jerusalem,
and may you live to see your children's children.

PSALM 128:1–6

The wife

A wife of noble character who can find?
She is worth far more than rubies.
Her husband has full confidence in her
and lacks nothing of value.
She brings him good, not harm,
all the days of her life.
She sets about her work vigorously;
her arms are strong for her tasks.
She opens her arms to the poor
and extends her hands to the needy.
When it snows, she has no fear for her household;
for all of them are clothed in scarlet.
She is clothed with strength and dignity;
she can laugh at the days to come.
She speaks with widsom,
and faithful instruction is on her tongue.
She watches over the affairs of her household
and does not eat the bread of idleness.
Charm is deceptive, and beauty is fleeting;
but a woman who fears the Lord is to be praised.
Give her the reward she has earned,
and let her works bring her praise at the city gate.

PROVERBS 31 (selection)

Wives, in the same way
    be submissive to your husbands
so that, if any of them do not believe the word,
they may be won over without talk
by the behaviour of their wives,
when they see the purity and reverence of your lives.

1 PETER 3:1,2

The father

Sons are a heritage from the Lord,
children a reward from him.
Like arrows in the hands of a warrior
are sons born in one's youth.   PSALM 127:3,4

Blessed is the man who fears the Lord,
who finds great delight in his commands.
His children will be mighty in the land;
each generation of the upright will be blessed.

PSALM 112:1,2

The jailer called for lights,
rushed in
and fell trembling before Paul and Silas.
He then brought them out and asked,
'Men, what must I do to be saved?'
They replied,
'Believe in the Lord Jesus,
and you will be saved –
you and your household.'
Then they spoke the word of the Lord to him
and to all the others in his house.
At that hour of the night
the jailer took them and washed their wounds;
then immediately he and all his family
        were baptised.
The jailer brought them into his house
and set a meal before them,
and the whole family was filled with joy,
because they had come to believe in God.   ACTS 16:29–34

The mother

O Lord, truly I am your servant;
I am your servant, the son of your maidservant.

PSALM 116:16

Hannah took the boy with her, young as he was. . .
and brought him to the house of the Lord at Shiloh.
When they had slaughtered the bull,
they brought the boy to Eli,
and she said to him,
'As surely as you live, my lord,
I am the woman who stood here beside you
    praying to the Lord.
I prayed for this child,
and the Lord has granted me what I asked of him.
So now I give him to the Lord.
For his whole life he shall be given over
    to the Lord.'

1 SAMUEL 1:24, 25–28

By faith Moses' parents hid him
    for three months after he was born,
because they saw he was no ordinary child,
and they were not afraid of the king's edict.

HEBREWS 11:23

I have been reminded of your sincere faith,
which first lived in your grandmother Lois
and in your mother Eunice
and, I am persuaded, now lives in you also.

2 TIMOTHY 1:5

The home

By wisdom a house is built,
and through understanding it is established;
through knowledge its rooms are filled
with rare and beautiful treasures.   PROVERBS 24:3,4

Not everyone who says to me, 'Lord, Lord,'
will enter the kingdom of heaven,
but only he who does the will of my Father
     who is in heaven.
Therefore everyone who hears these words of mine
and puts them into practice
is like a wise man who built his house on the rock.
The rain came down,
the streams rose,
and the winds blew and beat against that house;
yet it did not fall,
because it had its foundation on the rock.
But everyone who hears these words of mine
and does not put them into practice
is like a foolish man who built his house on sand.
The rain came down,
the streams rose,
and the winds blew and beat against that house,
and it fell with a great crash.   MATTHEW 7:21,24–27

Unless the Lord builds the house,
its builders labour in vain.   PSALM 127:1

The parent and the child

Train a child in the way he should go,
and when he is old he will not turn from it.   PROVERBS 22:6

Fathers,
do not exasperate your children;
instead,
bring them up in the training
    and instruction of the Lord.   EPHESIANS 6:4

I will open my mouth in parables,
I will utter things hidden from of old –
things we have heard and known,
things our fathers have told us.
We will not hide them from their children;
we will tell the next generation
the praiseworthy deeds of the Lord,
his power, and the wonders he has done.   PSALM 78:2–4

Continue in what you have learned
and have become convinced of,
because you know those from whom you learned it,
and how from infancy
you have known the holy Scriptures,
which are able to make you wise for salvation
through faith in Christ Jesus.
All Scripture is God-breathed
and is useful for teaching,
rebuking, correcting
and training in righteousness.   2 TIMOTHY 3:14–16

The child and the Lord

Eli realised
that the Lord was calling the boy.
So Eli told Samuel, 'Go and lie down,
and if he calls you, say,
"Speak, Lord, for your servant is listening." '
So Samuel went and lay down in his place.
The Lord came and stood there,
calling as at the other times, 'Samuel! Samuel!'
Then Samuel said,
'Speak, for your servant is listening.'
The Lord was with Samuel as he grew up,
and he let none of his words fall to the ground.
And all Israel from Dan to Beersheba
recognised that Samuel was attested
    as a prophet of the Lord.   1 SAMUEL 3:8–10,19,20

Jesus' mother said to him,
'Son, why have you treated us like this?
Your father and I have been anxiously searching
    for you.'
'Why were you searching for me?' he asked.
'Didn't you know I had to be in my Father's house?'
But they did not understand what he was saying to them.
Then he went down to Nazareth with them
and was obedient to them.
But his mother treasured all these things
    in her heart.
And Jesus grew in wisdom and stature,
and in favour with God and men.   LUKE 2:48–52

The parents' responsibility

He who spares the rod hates his son,
but he who loves him is careful to discipline him.

PROVERBS 13:24

The Lord said to Samuel:
'See, I am about to do something in Israel
that will make the ears of everyone
        who hears of it tingle.
At that time I will carry out against Eli
everything I spoke against his family –
from beginning to end.
For I told him that I would judge his family for ever
because of the sin he knew about;
his sons made themselves contemptible,
and he failed to restrain them.
Therefore, I swore to the house of Eli,
"The guilt of Eli's house will never be atoned for
        by sacrifice or offering." '

1 SAMUEL 3:11–14

I will set before my eyes no vile thing.
The deeds of faithless men I hate;
they shall not cling to me.
Men of perverse heart shall be far from me;
I will have nothing to do with evil.

PSALM 101:3,4

The elderly

And all the people
gave a great shout of praise to the Lord,
because the foundation of the house of the Lord
    was laid.
But many of the older priests and Levites
    and family heads,
who had seen the former temple,
wept aloud when they saw
    the foundation of this temple being laid,
while many others shouted for joy.
No-one could distinguish
    the sound of the shouts of joy
from the sound of weeping.   EZRA 3:11–13

For you have been my hope, O Sovereign Lord,
my confidence since my youth.
From birth I have relied on you;
you brought me forth from my mother's womb.
I will ever praise you.
I have become like a portent to many,
but you are my strong refuge.
Do not cast me away when I am old;
do not forsake me when my strength is gone.
Since my youth, O God, you have taught me,
and to this day I declare your marvellous deeds.
Even when I am old and grey,
do not forsake me, O God,
till I declare your power to the next generation,
your might to all who are to come.   PSALM 71:5–7,9,17,18

Hospitality

Do not forget to entertain strangers,
for by so doing
some people have entertained angels
without knowing it.   HEBREWS 13:2

When you give a luncheon or dinner,
do not invite your friends,
your brothers or relatives, or your rich neighbours;
if you do, they may invite you back
and so you will be repaid.
But when you give a banquet,
invite the poor, the crippled,
    the lame, the blind,
and you will be blessed.
Although they cannot repay you,
you will be repaid at the resurrection
    of the righteous.   LUKE 14:12–14

Be devoted to one another in brotherly love.
Honour one another above yourselves.
Share with God's people who are in need.
Practise hospitality.   ROMANS 12:10,13

He who receives you receives me,
and he who receives me
receives the one who sent me.
Anyone who receives a prophet
    because he is a prophet
will receive a prophet's reward. . .
And if anyone gives a cup of cold water
    to one of these little ones
because he is my disciple,
I tell you the truth,
he will certainly not lose his reward.   MATTHEW 10:40,41,42

Love each other deeply

The end of all things is near.
Therefore be clear minded and self-controlled
so that you can pray.
Above all, love each other deeply,
because love covers over a multitude of sins.
Offer hospitality to one another
        without grumbling.   1 PETER 4:7–9

Remind the people
to be subject to rulers and authorities,
to be obedient,
to be ready to do whatever is good,
to slander no-one,
to be peaceable and considerate,
and to show true humility towards all men.
At one time we too were foolish,
disobedient, deceived
and enslaved by all kinds of passions and pleasures.
We lived in malice and envy,
being hated and hating one another.
But when the kindness and love
        of God our Saviour appeared,
he saved us,
not because of righteous things we had done,
but because of his mercy. . .
And I want you to stress these things,
so that those who have trusted in God
may be careful to devote themselves
        to doing what is good.
These things are excellent
and profitable for everyone.   TITUS 3:1–5,8

Be strong and very courageous

After the death of Moses the servant of the Lord,
the Lord said to Joshua son of Nun, Moses' assistant:
'No-one will be able to stand up against you
all the days of your life.
As I was with Moses, so I will be with you;
I will never leave you or forsake you.
Be strong and very courageous.
Be careful to obey all the law
     my servant Moses gave you;
do not turn from it to the right or to the left,
that you may be successful wherever you go.' JOSHUA 1:1,5,7

Whatever happens,
conduct yourselves in a manner
     worthy of the gospel of Christ.
Then, whether I come and see you
or only hear about you in my absence,
I will know that you stand firm in one spirit,
contending as one man for the faith of the gospel
without being frightened in any way
     by those who oppose you.
This is a sign to them that they will be destroyed,
but that you will be saved – and that by God.
For it has been granted to you on behalf of Christ
not only to believe on him,
but also to suffer for him,
since you are going through the same struggle
     you saw I had,
and now hear that I still have.   PHILIPPIANS 1:27–30

We are not alone

David said to the Philistine,
'You come against me with sword and spear and javelin,
but I come against you in the name of the Lord Almighty,
the God of the armies of Israel,
whom you have defied.
This day the Lord will hand you over to me,
and I'll strike you down and cut off your head.
Today I will give the carcasses of the Philistine army
to the birds of the air and the beasts of the earth,
and the whole world will know
that there is a God in Israel.
All those gathered here will know
that it is not by sword or spear that the Lord saves;
for the battle is the Lord's,
and he will give all of you into our hands.'
As the Philistine moved closer to attack him,
David ran quickly towards the battle line to meet him.

1 SAMUEL 17:45–48

Now I know that the Lord saves his anointed;
he answers him from his holy heaven
with the saving power of his right hand.
Some trust in chariots and some in horses,
but we trust in the name of the Lord our God.
They are brought to their knees and fall,
but we rise up and stand firm.
O Lord, save the king!
Answer us when we call!　　　PSALM 20:6–9

We have a leader

Now when Joshua was near Jericho,
he looked up
and saw a man standing in front of him
with a drawn sword in his hand,
Joshua went up to him and asked,
'Are you for us or for our enemies?'
'Neither,' he replied,
'but as commander of the army of the Lord
    I have now come.'   JOSHUA 5:13,14

God is with us; he is our leader.
His priests with their trumpets
will sound the battle cry against you.
Men of Israel, do not fight against the Lord,
    the God of your fathers,
for you will not succeed.   2 CHRONICLES 13:12

I saw heaven standing open
and there before me was a white horse
whose rider is called Faithful and True.
With justice he judges and makes war.
His eyes are like blazing fire,
and on his head are many crowns. . .
The armies of heaven were following him,
riding on white horses
and dressed in fine linen, white and clean.
On his robe and on his thigh
he has this name written:
King of kings and Lord of lords.   REVELATION 19:11,12,14,16

Be prepared for opposition

Those who hate me without reason
outnumber the hairs of my head;
many are my enemies without cause,
those who seek to destroy me. . .
May those who hope in you
not be disgraced because of me,
O Lord, the Lord Almighty;
may those who seek you
not be put to shame because of me,
O God of Israel.
For I endure scorn for your sake,
and shame covers my face.
I am a stranger to my brothers,
an alien to my own mother's sons.   PSALM 69:4,6–8

I am sending you out
like sheep among wolves.
Therefore be as shrewd as snakes
and as innocent as doves.
But be on your guard against men;
they will hand you over to the local councils
and flog you in their synagogues.
But when they arrest you,
do not worry about what to say or how to say it.
At that time you will be given what to say,
for it will not be you speaking,
but the Spirit of your Father speaking through you.
Brother will betray brother to death,
and a father his child;
children will rebel against their parents
and have them put to death.
All men will hate you because of me,
but he who stands firm to the end will be saved.
          MATTHEW 10:16,17,19–22

Live in the world, but not by its standards

Trust in the Lord and do good;
dwell in the land and enjoy safe pasture.
Delight yourself in the Lord
and he will give you the desires of your heart.
Commit your way to the Lord;
trust in him and he will do this:
He will make your righteousness shine like the dawn,
the justice of your cause like the noonday sun.
Be still before the Lord and wait patiently for him;
do not fret when men succeed in their ways,
when they carry out their wicked schemes.
Refrain from anger and turn from wrath;
do not fret – it leads only to evil.   PSALM 37:3–8

Everyone who wants to live a godly life
    in Christ Jesus
will be persecuted,
while evil men and impostors
will go from bad to worse,
deceiving and being deceived.
But as for you,
continue in what you have learned
and have become convinced of. . .   2 TIMOTHY 3:12–14

For though we live in the world,
we do not wage war as the world does.
The weapons we fight with
are not the weapons of the world.
On the contrary,
they have divine power to demolish strongholds.
    2 CORINTHIANS 10:3,4

Be alert, be equipped

From that day on, half of my men did the work,
while the other half were equipped with spears,
    shields, bows and armour.
The officers posted themselves
behind all the people of Judah
    who were building the wall.
Those who carried materials
did their work with one hand
and held a weapon in the other,
and each of the builders wore his sword at his side
as he worked. . .   NEHEMIAH 4:16–18

Therefore put on the full armour of God,
so that when the day of evil comes,
you may be able to stand your ground,
and after you have done everything, to stand.
Stand firm then,
with the belt of truth buckled around your waist,
with the breastplate of righteousness in place,
and with your feet fitted with the readiness
that comes from the gospel of peace.
In addition to all this, take up the shield of faith,
with which you can extinguish
all the flaming arrows of the evil one.
Take the helmet of salvation
and the sword of the Spirit,
    which is the word of God.
And pray in the Spirit on all occasions
with all kinds of prayers and requests.
With this in mind, be alert
and always keep on praying for all the saints.
        EPHESIANS 6:13–18

The Christian battle requires effort

Do you not know that in a race
   all the runners run,
but only one gets the prize?
Run in such a way as to get the prize.
Everyone who competes in the games
   goes into strict training.
They do it to get a crown that will not last;
but we do it to get a crown that will last for ever.
Therefore I do not run like a man running aimlessly. . .

1 CORINTHIANS 9:24–26

I press on to take hold of that
   for which Christ Jesus took hold of me.
Brothers, I do not consider myself yet to have
   taken hold of it.
But one thing I do:
Forgetting what is behind
and straining towards what is ahead,
I press on towards the goal
to win the prize
for which God has called me heavenwards
   in Christ Jesus.   PHILIPPIANS 3:12–14

I have fought the good fight,
I have finished the race,
I have kept the faith.
Now there is in store for me
the crown of righteousness,
which the Lord, the righteous Judge,
will award to me on that day –
and not only to me,
but also to all who have longed for his appearing.

2 TIMOTHY 4:7,8

Suffering in the battle

Jesus then began to teach the disciples
that the Son of Man must suffer many things
and be rejected by the elders, chief priests
    and teachers of the law,
and that he must be killed
and after three days rise again.
'If anyone would come after me,
he must deny himself
and take up his cross and follow me.
For whoever wants to save his life will lose it,
but whoever loses his life for me and for the gospel
    will save it.'   MARK 8:31,34,35

Peter was hurt
because Jesus asked him the third time,
'Do you love me?'
He said, 'Lord,
you know all things;
you know that I love you.'
Jesus said, 'Feed my sheep.
I tell you the truth,
when you were younger you dressed yourself
and went where you wanted;
but when you are old
you will stretch out your hands,
and someone else will dress you
and lead you where you do not want to go.'
Jesus said this to indicate the kind of death
by which Peter would glorify God.
Then he said to him, 'Follow me!'   JOHN 21:17–19

Things are not as they seem

As servants of God
we commend ourselves in every way:
in great endurance;
in troubles, hardships and distresses;
in beatings, imprisonments and riots;
in hard work, sleepless nights and hunger;
through glory and dishonour,
bad report and good report;
genuine, yet regarded as impostors;
known, yet regarded as unknown;
dying, and yet we live on;
beaten, and yet not killed;
sorrowful, yet always rejoicing;
poor, yet making many rich;
having nothing,
and yet possessing everything. 2 CORINTHIANS 6:4,5,8–10

Looking at his disciples, Jesus said:
'Blessed are you who are poor,
for yours is the kingdom of God.
Blessed are you who hunger now,
for you will be satisfied.
Blessed are you who weep now,
for you will laugh.
Blessed are you when men hate you,
when they exclude you and insult you
and reject your name as evil,
      because of the Son of Man.
Rejoice in that day and leap for joy;
because great is your reward in heaven.
For that is how their fathers treated the prophets.'
                                                LUKE 6:20–23

The example Jesus set

Dear friends,
do not be surprised
at the painful trial you are suffering,
as though something strange were happening to you.
But rejoice that you participate
in the sufferings of Christ,
so that you may be overjoyed when his glory is revealed.
If you are insulted because of the name of Christ,
you are blessed,
for the Spirit of glory and of God rests on you.

1 PETER 4:12–14

He was oppressed and afflicted,
yet he did not open his mouth;
he was led like a lamb to the slaughter,
and as a sheep before her shearers is silent,
so he did not open his mouth.
By oppression and judgement, he was taken away.
And who can speak of his descendants?
For he was cut off from the land of the living;
for the transgression of my people he was stricken.
He was assigned a grave with the wicked,
and with the rich in his death,
though he had done no violence,
nor was any deceit in his mouth.

ISAIAH 53:7–9

Blessed are those who are persecuted
        because of righteousness,
for theirs is the kingdom of heaven.

MATTHEW 5:10

The suffering of Christ

Those who passed by hurled insults at him,
shaking their heads and saying,
'You who are going to destroy the temple
and build it in three days,
save yourself!
Come down from the cross,
if you are the Son of God!'
In the same way the chief priests,
the teachers of the law and the elders mocked him.
'He trusts in God.
Let God rescue him now if he wants him,
for he said, "I am the Son of God." '   MATTHEW 27:39–41,43

When they hurled their insults at him,
he did not retaliate;
when he suffered,
he made no threats.
Instead, he entrusted himself to him
        who judges justly.   1 PETER 2:23

All who see me mock me;
they hurl insults, shaking their heads:
'He trusts in the Lord; let the Lord rescue him.
Let him deliver him, since he delights in him.'   PSALM 22:7,8

Consider him
who endured such opposition from sinful men,
so that you will not grow weary
and lose heart.
In your struggle against sin,
you have not yet resisted
to the point of shedding your blood.   HEBREWS 12:3,4

Be assured of the outcome

Who will bring any charge
against those whom God has chosen?
It is God who justifies.
Who is he that condemns?
Christ Jesus, who died –
more than that, who was raised to life –
is at the right hand of God
and is also interceding for us.
Who shall separate us from the love of Christ?
Shall trouble or hardship
or persecution or famine
or nakedness or danger or sword?
No, in all these things we are more than conquerors
through him who loved us. ROMANS 8:33–35,37

Because the Sovereign Lord helps me,
I will not be disgraced.
Therefore have I set my face like flint,
and I know I will not be put to shame.
He who vindicates me is near.
Who then will bring charges against me?
Let us face each other!
Who is my accuser?
Let him confront me!
It is the Sovereign Lord who helps me.
Who is he that will condemn me?
They will all wear out like a garment;
the moths will eat them up.
Who among you fears the Lord
and obeys the word of his servant?
Let him who walks in the dark,
who has no light,
trust in the name of the Lord and rely on his God.

ISAIAH 50:7–10

Heaven is our reward

Stephen,
full of the Holy Spirit,
looked up to heaven and saw the glory of God,
and Jesus standing at the right hand of God.
'Look,' he said,
'I see heaven open
and the Son of Man standing at the right hand of God.'
At this they covered their ears and,
yelling at the top of their voices,
they all rushed at him,
dragged him out of the city
and began to stone him.
While they were stoning him,
Stephen prayed, 'Lord Jesus, receive my spirit.'
Then he fell on his knees and cried out,
'Lord, do not hold this sin against them.'
When he had said this,
he fell asleep.   ACTS 7:55–58,59,60

Blessed are you
when people insult you,
persecute you
and falsely say all kinds of evil against you
because of me.
Rejoice and be glad,
because great is your reward in heaven,
for in the same way they persecuted the prophets
who were before you.   MATTHEW 5:11,12

The voice from heaven

The voice of the Lord is over the waters;
the God of glory thunders,
the Lord thunders over the mighty waters.
The voice of the Lord is powerful;
the voice of the Lord is majestic.
The voice of the Lord breaks the cedars;
the Lord breaks in pieces the cedars of Lebanon.
The voice of the Lord strikes
with flashes of lightning.
The voice of the Lord twists the oaks
and strips the forests bare.
And in his temple all cry, 'Glory!'   PSALM 29:3-5,7,9

Jesus was transfigured before them.
His face shone like the sun,
and his clothes became as white as the light...
A bright cloud enveloped them,
and a voice from the cloud said,
'This is my Son, whom I love;
with him I am well pleased.
Listen to him!'   MATTHEW 17:2,5

See to it that you do not refuse him who speaks.
If they did not escape
when they refused him who warned them on earth,
how much less will we,
if we turn away from him who warns us from heaven?
HEBREWS 12:25

The eternal Lord

In the beginning was the Word,
and the Word was with God,
and the Word was God.
He was with God in the beginning.
Through him all things were made;
without him nothing was made
     that has been made.
In him was life,
and that life was the light of men.
The light shines in the darkness,
but the darkness has not understood it.
The Word became flesh
and lived for a while among us.
We have seen his glory,
the glory of the one and only Son,
who came from the Father,
full of grace and truth.   JOHN 1:1–5,14

He is the image of the invisible God,
the firstborn over all creation.
For by him all things were created:
things in heaven and on earth,
visible and invisible,
whether thrones or powers
or rulers or authorities;
all things were created by him and for him.
He is before all things,
and in him all things hold together.
For God was pleased to have
     all his fullness dwell in him.   COLOSSIANS 1:15–17,19

The living one

Then King Nebuchadnezzar
leaped to his feet in amazement
and asked his advisers,
'Wasn't it three men that we tied up
and threw into the fire?'
They replied, 'Certainly, O king.'
He said, 'Look!
I see four men walking around in the fire,
unbound and unharmed,
and the fourth looks like a son of the gods.' DANIEL 3:24,25

His face was like the sun
shining in all its brilliance.
When I saw him, I fell at his feet as though dead.
Then he placed his right hand on me and said:
'Do not be afraid.
I am the First and the Last.
I am the Living One.' REVELATION 1:16–18

And we, who with unveiled faces
all reflect the Lord's glory,
are being transformed into his likeness
with ever increasing glory,
which comes from the Lord, who is the Spirit.
2 CORINTHIANS 3:18

But our citizenship is in heaven.
And we eagerly await a Saviour from there,
the Lord Jesus Christ. . .
who will transform our lowly bodies
so that they will be like his glorious body.
PHILIPPIANS 3:20,21

The brilliant vision

I looked up
and there before me
was a man dressed in linen,
with a belt of the finest gold
    around his waist. . .
His face was like lightning,
his eyes like flaming torches. . .
and his voice
like the sound of a multitude.
. . . The men with me did not see it,
but such terror overwhelmed them
that they fled and hid themselves.
Then I heard him speaking,
and as I listened to him,
I fell into a deep sleep,
my face to the ground.
A hand touched me and set me trembling
    on my hands and knees.
He said, 'Daniel, you who are highly esteemed,
consider carefully the words I am about to speak
    to you.'
              DANIEL 10:5,6,7,9–11

Suddenly a light from heaven flashed around him.
He fell to the ground
and heard a voice say to him,
'Saul, Saul, why do you persecute me?'
'Who are you, Lord?' Saul asked.
'I am Jesus, whom you are persecuting,'
he replied.
'Now get up and go into the city,
and you will be told what you must do.'
The men travelling with Saul stood there speechless;
they heard the sound but did not see anyone.
Saul got up from the ground,
but when he opened his eyes he could see nothing.
              ACTS 9:3–8

Noah – his godliness

He did not spare the ancient world
when he brought the flood
    on its ungodly people,
but protected Noah,
a preacher of righteousness,
and seven others.   2 PETER 2:5

The Lord saw
how great man's wickedness on the earth
    had become,
and that every inclination of the thoughts
    of his heart
was only evil all the time.
So the Lord said,
'I will wipe mankind, whom I have created,
off from the face of the earth . . .
for I am grieved that I have made them.'
But Noah found favour in the eyes of the Lord. . .
Noah was a righteous man,
blameless among the people of his time,
and he walked with God.   GENESIS 6:5,7,8,9

The fool says in his heart,
'There is no God.'
They are corrupt, and their ways are vile;
there is no-one who does good.
God looks down from heaven on the sons of men
to see if there are any who understand,
any who seek God.
Will the evildoers never learn –
those who devour my people as men eat bread
and who do not call on God?
There they were,
overwhelmed with dread,
where there was nothing to dread.   PSALM 53:1,2,4,5

Noah – his obedience

God said to Noah,
'I am going to put an end to all people,
for the earth is filled with violence
    because of them.
I am surely going to destroy both them and the earth.
So make yourself an ark of cypress wood. . .
I am going to bring floodwaters on the earth
to destroy all life under the heavens,
every creature that has the breath of life in it.
Everything on earth will perish.
But I will establish my covenant with you,
and you will enter the ark –
you and your sons and your wife
    and your sons' wives
with you.   GENESIS 6:13,14,17,18

By faith Noah,
when warned about things not yet seen,
in holy fear built an ark
    to save his family.
By his faith he condemned the world
and became heir of the righteousness
    that comes by faith.   HEBREWS 11:7

Just as it was in the days of Noah,
so also will it be in the days of the Son of Man.
People were eating, drinking,
marrying and being given in marriage
up to the day Noah entered the ark.
Then the flood came and destroyed them all.
                                              LUKE 17:26,27

Lot – rescued

When Lot hesitated,
the men grasped his hand
and the hands of his wife and of his two daughters
and led them safely out of the city,
for the Lord was merciful to them.
As soon as they had brought them out,
one of them said,
'Flee for your lives!
Don't look back,
and don't stop anywhere in the plain!
Flee to the mountains
or you will be swept away!'
By the time Lot reached Zoar,
the sun had risen over the land.
Then the Lord rained down burning sulphur
on Sodom and Gomorrah.   GENESIS 19:16,17,23,24

God condemned the cities of Sodom and Gomorrah
by burning them to ashes,
and made them an example
      of what is going to happen to the ungodly;
and if he rescued Lot, a righteous man,
who was distressed by the filthy lives
      of lawless men . . .
if this is so, then the Lord knows
      how to rescue godly men from trials.   2 PETER 2:6,7,9

It was the same in the days of Lot.
People were eating and drinking,
buying and selling, planting and building.
But the day Lot left Sodom,
fire and sulphur rained down from heaven
and destroyed them all.
It will be just like this
on the day the Son of Man is revealed.   LUKE 17:28–30

Abraham – his faith

The Lord had said to Abram,
'Leave your country,
  your people and your father's household
and go to the land I will show you.'   GENESIS 12:1

By faith Abraham,
when called to go to a place
he would later receive as his inheritance,
obeyed and went,
even though he did not know
      where he was going.   HEBREWS 11:8

Then God said 'Take your son,
your only son Isaac, whom you love,
and go to the region of Moriah.
Sacrifice him there as a burnt offering. . .'
Abraham reached out his hand
and took the knife to slay his son.   GENESIS 22:2,10

By faith Abraham,
when God tested him,
offered Isaac as a sacrifice.   HEBREWS 11:17

Jeremiah – God's unpopular man

The officials said to the king,
   'This man should be put to death. . .'
'He is in your hands,' King Zedekiah answered.
'The king can do nothing to oppose you.'
So they took Jeremiah
and put him into the cistern of Malkijah,
   the king's son,
which was in the courtyard of the guard.
They lowered Jeremiah by ropes into the cistern;
it had no water in it, only mud,
and Jeremiah sank down into the mud.   JEREMIAH 38:4,5,6

Save me, O God,
for the waters have come up to my neck.
I sink in the miry depths . . .
I am worn out calling for help;
my throat is parched . . .
In your great love, O God,
answer me with your sure salvation.
Rescue me from the mire,
do not let me sink;
deliver me from those who hate me.
Do not hide your face from your servant;
answer me quickly, for I am in trouble.   PSALM 69:1,3,13,

While the king was sitting in the Benjamin Gate,
Ebed-Melech went out of the palace and said to him,
'My lord the king,
these men have acted wickedly
in all they have done to Jeremiah the prophet.
They have thrown him into a cistern,
where he will starve to death . . .'
Then the king commanded Ebed-Melech. . .
'Take thirty men from here with you
and lift Jeremiah the prophet out of the cistern
   before he dies.'   JEREMIAH 38:8,9,10

Job – God's patient man

Job replied,
'You are talking like a foolish woman.
Shall we accept good from God,
and not trouble?'
In all this,
Job did not sin in what he said.   JOB 2:10

Be patient, then, brothers,
    until the Lord's coming. . .
As an example of patience
    in the face of suffering,
take the prophets
who spoke in the name of the Lord.
As you know,
we consider blessed those who have persevered.
You have heard of Job's perseverance
and have seen what the Lord finally brought about.
The Lord is full of compassion and mercy.
          JAMES 5:7,10,11

After Job had prayed for his friends,
the Lord made him prosperous again
and gave him twice as much as he had before.
The Lord blessed the latter part of Job's life
more than the first.   JOB 42:10,12

Daniel – his faithfulness

My enemies speak against me;
those who wait to kill me conspire together.
They say, 'God has forsaken him;
pursue him and seize him,
for no-one will rescue him.'
May my accusers perish in shame. . .
But as for me, I shall always have hope;
I will praise you more and more.
My mouth will tell of your righteousness,
of your salvation all day long.   PSALM 71:10,11,13,14,15

Finally these men said,
'We will never find any basis
for charges against this man Daniel
unless it has something to do
     with the law of his God.'
So the administrators and the satraps
went as a group to the king and said:
'O King Darius . . .
issue an edict and enforce the decree
that anyone who prays to any god or man
during the next thirty days,
except to you, O king,
shall be thrown into the lions' den.'
Now when Daniel learned that the decree
had been published,
he went home to his upstairs room
where the window opened towards Jerusalem.
Three times a day he got down on his knees
     and prayed,
giving thanks to his God,
just as he had done before.   DANIEL 6:5,6,7,10

Paul – Christ's converted man

They all rushed at him,
dragged him out of the city and began to stone him.
Meanwhile, the witnesses laid their clothes
at the feet of a young man named Saul.
While they were stoning him,
Stephen prayed,
'Lord Jesus, receive my spirit.'
Then he fell on his knees and cried out,
'Lord, do not hold this sin against them.'
When he had said this, he fell asleep.
And Saul was there, giving approval to his death.

ACTS 7:58–8:1

Saul was still breathing out murderous threats
    against the Lord's disciples.
He went to the high priest
and asked him for letters
    to the synagogues in Damascus,
so that if he found any there
    who belonged to the Way,
whether men or women,
he might take them as prisoners to Jerusalem.

ACTS 9:1,2

I thank Christ Jesus our Lord,
who has given me strength,
that he considered me faithful,
appointing me to his service.
Even though I was once a blasphemer
    and a persecutor and a violent man,
I was shown mercy.   1 TIMOTHY 1:12,13

Paul – called by God

You have heard . . .
how intensely I persecuted the church of God
and tried to destroy it.
But God, who set me apart from birth
and called me by his grace,
was pleased to reveal his Son in me
so that I might preach him
    among the Gentiles.   GALATIANS 1:13,15,16

Lord, you created my inmost being;
you knit me together in my mother's womb.
I praise you because I am fearfully and wonderfully made;
your works are wonderful, I know that full well.
My frame was not hidden from you
    when I was made in the secret place.
When I was woven together in the depths of the earth,
your eyes saw my unformed body.
All the days ordained for me
were written in your book
    before one of them came to be.
How precious to me are your thoughts, O God!
How vast is the sum of them!
Were I to count them,
they would outnumber the grains of sand.
When I awake,
I am still with you.   PSALM 139:13–18

Mary – God's chosen woman

The angel answered,
'The Holy Spirit will come upon you,
  and the power of the Most High will overshadow you.
So the holy one to be born will be called
      the Son of God.'
'I am the Lord's servant,' Mary answered.
'May it be to me as you have said.'
Then the angel left her.   LUKE 1:35,38

So they hurried off
and found Mary and Joseph,
and the baby, who was lying in the manger.
When they had seen him,
they spread the word concerning
      what had been told them about this child,
and all who heard it
were amazed at what the shepherds said to them.
But Mary treasured up all these things
and pondered them in her heart.   LUKE 2:16–19

Jesus' mother said to him,
'Son, why have you treated us like this?
Your father and I have been
      anxiously searching for you.'
'Why were you searching for me?'
he asked.
'Didn't you know
      I had to be in my Father's house?'
His mother treasured all these things
in her heart.   LUKE 2:48,49,51

Mary – favoured by God

The angel went to her and said,
'Greetings, you who are highly favoured!
The Lord is with you.'
Mary was greatly troubled at his words
and wondered what kind of greeting this might be.
But the angel said to her,
'Do not be afraid, Mary,
you have found favour with God.
You will be with child and give birth to a son,
and you are to give him the name Jesus.
He will be great
and will be called the Son of the Most High.'

LUKE 1:28–32

Jesus' mother said to him,
'They have no more wine.'
'Dear woman, why do you involve me?'
Jesus replied,
'My time has not yet come.'
His mother said to the servants,
'Do whatever he tells you.'
This,
the first of his miraculous signs,
Jesus performed in Cana of Galilee.
He thus revealed his glory,
and his disciples put their faith in him.
After this he went down to Capernaum
with his mother and brothers and his disciples.

JOHN 2:3-5,11,12

Aquila and Priscilla – the couple God used

Paul left Athens and went to Corinth.
There he met a Jew named Aquila,
a native of Pontus,
who had recently come from Italy
　　with his wife Priscilla. . .
Paul went to see them,
and because he was a tentmaker as they were,
he stayed and worked with them.　　　ACTS 18:1,2,3

Aquila and Priscilla
greet you warmly in the Lord,
and so does the church that meets at their house.
　　　　　　　　　　　　　1 CORINTHIANS 16:19

A Jew named Apollos . . . came to Ephesus.
He knew only the baptism of John.
He began to speak boldly in the synagogue.
When Priscilla and Aquila heard him,
they invited him to their home
and explained to him the way of God
　　more adequately.
Apollos wanted to go to Achaia. . .
On arriving, he was a great help
　　to those who by grace had believed.　　ACTS 18:24,25,26,27

Greet Priscilla and Aquila,
my fellow-workers in Christ Jesus.
They risked their lives for me.
Not only I but all the churches of the Gentiles
　　are grateful to them.
Greet also the church that meets at their house.
　　　　　　　　　　　　　ROMANS 16:3–5

Righteousness

The sinners of Zion are terrified;
trembling grips the godless:
'Who of us can dwell with the consuming fire?
Who of us can dwell with everlasting burning?'
He who walks righteously and speaks what is right,
who rejects gain from extortion
and keeps his hand from accepting bribes,
who stops his ears against plots of murder
and shuts his eyes against contemplating evil –
this is the man who will dwell on the heights,
whose refuge will be the mountain fortress.
His bread will be supplied,
and water will not fail him.   ISAIAH 33:14–16

Blessed is he who has regard for the weak;
the Lord delivers him in times of trouble.
The Lord will protect him and preserve his life;
he will bless him in the land
and not surrender him to the desire of his foes.
The Lord will sustain him on his sickbed
and restore him from his bed of illness.   PSALM 41:1–3

Who is going to harm you
        if you are eager to do good?
But even if you should suffer for what is right,
you are blessed.   1 PETER 3:13,14

Justice

You hate the one who reproves in court
and despise him who tells the truth.
You trample on the poor
and force him to give you corn.
Therefore, though you have built stone mansions,
you will not live in them;
though you have planted lush vineyards,
you will not drink their wine.
For I know how many are your offences
and how great your sins.
You oppress the righteous and take bribes
and you deprive the poor of justice in the courts.
Therefore the prudent man keeps quiet in such times,
for the times are evil.
Seek good, not evil, that you may live.
Then the Lord God Almighty will be with you,
just as you say he is.
Hate evil, love good; maintain justice in the courts.
Perhaps the Lord God Almighty will have mercy
      on the remnant of Joseph.   AMOS 5:10–15

Is not this the kind of fasting I have chosen:
to loose the chains of injustice
and untie the cords of the yoke,
to set the oppressed free and break every yoke?
Is it not to share your food with the hungry
and to provide the poor wanderer with shelter –
when you see the naked, to clothe him,
and not to turn away from your own flesh and blood?
Then your light will break forth like the dawn,
and your healing will quickly appear;
then your righteousness will go before you,
and the glory of the Lord will be your rearguard.
      ISAIAH 58:6–8

Impartial behaviour

Do not pervert justice;
do not show partiality to the poor
or favouritism to the great,
but judge your neighbour fairly.
Do not go about spreading slander among your people.
Do not do anything that endangers
    your neighbour's life.
I am the Lord.
Do not hate your brother in your heart.
Rebuke your neighbour frankly
so that you will not share in his guilt.
Do not seek revenge
or bear a grudge against one of your people,
but love your neighbour as yourself.
I am the Lord.   LEVITICUS 19:15–18

You have heard
that it was said to the people long ago,
'Do not murder,
and anyone who murders will be the subject to judgement.'
But I tell you
that anyone who is angry
with his brother
will be subject to judgement.
Therefore,
if you are offering your gift at the altar
and there remember
that your brother has something against you,
leave the gift there in front of the altar.
First go and be reconciled to your brother;
then come and offer your gift.   MATTHEW 5:21,22,23,24

Compassion

Ruth the Moabitess said to Naomi,
'Let me go to the fields
and pick up the leftover grain
behind anyone in whose eyes I find favour. . .'
So she went out
and began to glean in the fields
behind the harvesters. . .   RUTH 2:2,3

When you reap the harvest of your land,
do not reap to the very edges of your field
or gather the gleanings of your harvest.
Do not go over your vineyard a second time
or pick up the grapes that have fallen.
Leave them for the poor and the alien.
I am the Lord your God.   LEVITICUS 19:9,10

If there is a poor man among your brothers
in any of the towns of the land
that the Lord your God is giving you,
do not be hard-hearted or tight-fisted
     towards your poor brother.
Rather be open-handed
and freely lend him whatever he needs.
Give generously to him
and do so without a grudging heart;
then because of this
the Lord your God will bless you in all your work
and in everything you put your hand to.
                          DEUTERONOMY 15:7,8,10

Compassion

Then the King will say to those on his right,
'Come, you who are blessed by my Father;
take your inheritance,
the kingdom prepared for you
since the creation of the world.
For I was hungry and you gave me something to eat,
I was thirsty and you gave me something to drink,
I was a stranger and you invited me in,
I needed clothes and you clothed me,
I was sick and you looked after me,
I was in prison and you came to visit me.'
Then the righteous will answer him,
'Lord, when did we see you hungry and feed you. . .?'
The King will reply,
'I tell you the truth,
whatever you did
for one of the least of these brothers of mine,
you did for me.'   MATTHEW 25:34–37,40

Keep on loving each other as brothers.
Do not forget to entertain strangers,
for by so doing
some people have entertained angels
without knowing it.
Remember those in prison
as if you were their fellow prisoners,
and those who are ill-treated
as if you yourselves were suffering.   HEBREWS 13:1–3

Forgiveness and restraint

Love your enemies,
do good to those who hate you,
bless those who curse you,
pray for those who ill-treat you.
If you love those who love you,
what credit is that to you?
Even 'sinners' love those who love them.
And if you do good to those who are good to you,
what credit is that to you?
Even 'sinners' do that.
Be merciful, just as your Father is merciful.

LUKE 6:27,28,32,33,36

Do not repay anyone evil for evil.
Be careful to do what is right
    in the eyes of everybody.
If it is possible,
as far as it depends on you,
live at peace with everyone.
Do not take revenge, my friends,
but leave room for God's wrath,
for it is written:
'It is mine to avenge; I will repay,'
    says the Lord.
On the contrary:
'If your enemy is hungry, feed him;
if he is thirsty, give him something to drink.
In doing this, you will heap burning coals
    on his head.'
Do not be overcome by evil,
but overcome evil with good.

ROMANS 12:17–21

Generosity

Even in darkness light dawns for the upright,
for the gracious and compassionate and righteous man.
Good will come to him who is generous
    and lends freely,
who conducts his affairs with justice.
Surely he will never be shaken;
a righteous man will be remembered for ever.
He has scattered abroad his gifts to the poor,
his righteousness endures for ever;
his horn will be lifted high in honour.   PSALM 112:4–6,9

The wicked borrow and do not repay,
but the righteous give generously;
those the Lord blesses will inherit the land,
but those he curses will be cut off.   PSALM 37:21,22

If one of your countrymen becomes poor
and is unable to support himself among you,
help him as you would an alien
    or a temporary resident,
so that he can continue to live among you.
Do not take interest of any kind from him,
but fear your God,
so that your countryman
    may continue to live among you.
You must not lend him money at interest
or sell him food at a profit.
I am the Lord your God, who brought you out of Egypt
to give you the land of Canaan
and to be your God.   LEVITICUS 25:35–38

Mutual concern

My brothers,
as believers in our glorious Lord Jesus Christ,
don't show favouritism.   JAMES 2:1

And now, brothers,
we want you to know about the grace
that God has given the Macedonian churches.
Out of the most severe trial,
their overflowing joy and their extreme poverty
        welled up in rich generosity.
For I testify
that they gave as much as they were able,
and even beyond their ability.
Entirely on their own,
they urgently pleaded with us
for the privilege of sharing in this service
        to the saints.
And they did not do as we expected,
but they gave themselves first to the Lord
and then to us in keeping with God's will.
                                    2 CORINTHIANS 8:1–5

Listen, my dear brothers:
Has not God chosen those
        who are poor in the eyes of the world
to be rich in faith
and to inherit the kingdom he promised those
        who love him?
But you have insulted the poor.   JAMES 2:5,6

Wealth can bring complacency!

There was a rich man
who was dressed in purple and fine linen
and lived in luxury every day.
At his gate was laid a beggar named Lazarus,
covered with sores
and longing to eat what fell from the rich man's table.
Even the dogs came and licked his sores.
The time came when the beggar died
and the angels carried him to Abraham's side.
The rich man also died and was buried.
In hell, where he was in torment,
he looked up and saw Abraham far away,
    with Lazarus by his side.
So he called to him,
'Father Abraham, have pity on me
and send Lazarus to dip the tip of his finger in water
    and cool my tongue,
because I am in agony in this fire.'   LUKE 16:19–24

Israel grew fat and kicked;
filled with food, he became heavy and sleek.
He abandoned the God who made him
and rejected the Rock his Saviour.
They made him jealous with their foreign gods
and angered him with their detestable idols.
They sacrificed to demons, which are not God –
gods they had not known,
gods that recently appeared,
gods your fathers did not fear.
You deserted the Rock, who fathered you;
you forgot the God who gave you birth.
                              DEUTERONOMY 32:15–18

The proper use of wealth

If anyone has material possessions
and sees his brother in need
but has no pity on him,
how can the love of God be in him?
Dear children,
let us not love with words or tongue
but with actions and in truth.   1 JOHN 3:17,18

For you know the grace of our Lord Jesus Christ,
that though he was rich,
yet for your sakes he became poor,
so that you through his poverty might become rich.

     2 CORINTHIANS 8:9

Now listen, you rich people,
weep and wail
because of the misery that is coming upon you.
Your wealth has rotted,
and moths have eaten your clothes.
Your gold and silver are corroded.
Their corrosion will testify against you
and eat your flesh like fire.
You have hoarded wealth in the last days.
You have lived on earth in luxury and self-indulgence.
You have fattened yourselves in the day of slaughter.

     JAMES 5:1–3,5

Christian sacrifice

'All these commandments I have kept,'
the young man said.
'What do I still lack?'
Jesus answered,
'If you want to be perfect,
go, sell your possessions and give to the poor,
and you will have treasure in heaven.
Then come, follow me.'
When the young man heard this,
he went away sad,
because he had great wealth.
Then Jesus said to his disciples,
'I tell you the truth,
it is hard for a rich man
to enter the kingdom of heaven.
Again I tell you,
it is easier for a camel to go through
        the eye of a needle
than for a rich man to enter the kingdom of God.'

                                    MATTHEW 19:20–24

Do not be afraid, little flock,
for your Father has been pleased
        to give you the kingdom.
Sell your possessions and give to the poor.
Provide purses for yourselves that will not wear out,
a treasure in heaven that will not be exhausted,
where no thief comes near
and no moth destroys.
For where your treasure is,
there your heart will be also.   LUKE 12:32–34

Working faithfully

Slaves,
obey your earthly masters in everything;
and do it,
not only when their eye is on you
    and to win their favour,
but with sincerity of heart and reverence for the Lord.
Whatever you do,
work at it with all your heart,
as working for the Lord, not for men. . .
It is the Lord Christ you are serving. COLOSSIANS 3:22,23,24

The man with the two talents also came.
'Master,' he said,
'you entrusted me with two talents;
see, I have gained two more.'
His master replied,
'Well done, good and faithful servant!
You have been faithful with a few things;
I will put you in charge of many things.
Come and share your master's happiness!'
Then the man who had received the one talent came.
'Master,' he said,
'I knew that you are a hard man,
harvesting where you have not sown
and gathering where you have not scattered seed.
So I was afraid
and went out and hid your talent in the ground.
See, here is what belongs to you.'
His master replied,
'You wicked, lazy servant!' MATTHEW 25:22–26

The fair master

Slaves,
obey your earthly masters with respect and fear. . .
And masters,
treat your slaves in the same way.
Do not threaten them, since you know
that he who is both their Master and yours
    is in heaven,
and there is no favouritism with him.   EPHESIANS 6:5,9

I appeal to you for my son Onesimus
who became my son while I was in chains.
Perhaps the reason he was separated from you
    for a little while
was that you might have him back for good –
no longer as a slave,
but better than a slave, as a dear brother.
He is very dear to me but even dearer to you,
both as a man and as a brother in the Lord.
    PHILEMON 10,15,16

Here there is no Greek or Jew,
circumcised or uncircumcised,
barbarian, Scythian, slave or free,
but Christ is all, and is in all.
Therefore, as God's chosen people,
holy and dearly loved,
clothe yourselves with compassion, kindness,
humility, gentleness and patience.
Bear with each other
and forgive whatever grievances you may have
    against one another.
Forgive as the Lord forgave you.   COLOSSIANS 3:11–13

The responsibilities of leadership

The earlier governors – those preceding me –
placed a heavy burden on the people
and took forty shekels of silver from them
    in addition to food and wine.
Their assistants also lorded it over the people.
But out of reverence for God I did not act like that.
Instead, I devoted myself to the work on this wall.
All my men were assembled there for the work;
we did not acquire any land.   NEHEMIAH 5:15,16

'Woe to him who builds his palace by unrighteousness,
his upper rooms by injustice,
making his countrymen work for nothing,
not paying them for their labour.
He says, "I will build myself a great palace
    with spacious upper rooms."
So he makes large windows in it,
panels it with cedar and decorates it in red.
Does it make you a king to have more and more cedar?
Did not your father have food and drink?
He did what was right and just,
so all went well with him.
He defended the cause of the poor and needy,
and so all went well.
Is that not what it means to know me?'
    declares the Lord.   JEREMIAH 22:13–16

Civic and political responsibility

Remind the people
to be subject to rulers and authorities,
to be obedient,
to be ready to do whatever is good,
to slander no-one,
to be peaceable and considerate,
and to show true humility towards all men.   TITUS 3:1,2

Live such good lives among the pagans that,
though they accuse you of doing wrong,
they may see your good deeds
and glorify God on the day he visits us.
Submit yourselves for the Lord's sake
to every authority instituted among men:
whether to the king, as the supreme authority,
or to governors,
who are sent by him to punish those who do wrong
     and to commend those who do right.
For it is God's will that by doing good
you should silence the ignorant talk of foolish men.
Live as free men,
but do not use your freedom as a cover-up for evil;
live as servants of God.
Show proper respect to everyone:
Love the brotherhood of believers,
fear God,
honour the king.   1 PETER 2:12–17

The authorities are established by God

This is what the Lord says to his anointed,
to Cyrus, whose right hand I take hold of
to subdue nations before him
and to strip kings of their armour,
to open doors before him
so that gates will not be shut:
For the sake of Jacob my servant,
     of Israel my chosen,
I call you by name
and bestow on you a title of honour,
though you do not acknowledge me.
I am the Lord, and there is no other;
apart from me there is no God.
I will strengthen you,
though you have not acknowledged me.   ISAIAH 45:1,4,5

Everyone must submit himself
to the governing authorities,
for there is no authority
except that which God has established.
The authorities that exist have been established by God.
Consequently, he who rebels against the authority
is rebelling against what God has instituted,
and those who do so will bring judgement on themselves.
For rulers hold no terror for those who do right,
but for those who do wrong.
Do you want to be free from fear
     of the one in authority?
Then do what is right and he will commend you.
For he is God's servant to do you good.
But if you do wrong, be afraid,
for he does not bear the sword for nothing.
He is God's servant, an agent of wrath
to bring punishment on the wrongdoer.   ROMANS 13:1–4

Care for the alien

The Lord your God is God of gods
      and Lord of lords,
and great God, mighty and awesome,
who shows no partiality and accepts no bribes.
He defends the cause of the fatherless and the widow,
and loves the alien, giving him food and clothing.
And you are to love those who are aliens,
for you yourselves were aliens in Egypt.

DEUTERONOMY 10:17–19

O Lord, God of Israel. . .
as for the foreigner
who does not belong to your people Israel
but has come from a distant land
because of your great name and your mighty hand
and your outstretched arm –
when he comes and prays towards this temple,
then hear from heaven, your dwelling-place,
and do whatever the foreigner asks of you,
so that all the peoples of the earth
may know your name and fear you. . .

2 CHRONICLES 6:14,32,33

Philip met an Ethiopian eunuch. . .
who had gone to Jerusalem to worship,
and on his way home was sitting in his chariot
      reading the book of Isaiah the prophet.
The Spirit told Philip,
'Go to that chariot and stay near it.'
Then Philip ran up to the chariot
and heard the man reading Isaiah the prophet.
'Do you understand what you are reading?' Philip asked.
'How can I,' he said,
'unless someone explains it to me?'

ACTS 8:27,28–31

Respect for proper authority

'Teacher,' they said,
'we know you are a man of integrity
and that you teach the way of God
    in accordance with the truth.
You aren't swayed by men,
because you pay no attention to who they are.
Tell us then, what is your opinion?
Is it right to pay taxes to Caesar or not?'
But Jesus, knowing their evil intent, said,
'You hypocrites, why are you trying to trap me?
Show me the coin used for paying the tax.'
They brought him a denarius, and he asked them,
'Whose portrait is this? And whose inscription?'
'Caesar's,' they replied.
Then he said to them,
'Give to Caesar what is Caesar's,
and to God what is God's.'　　MATTHEW 22:16–21

It is necessary to submit to the authorities,
not only because of possible punishment
but also because of conscience.
This is also why you pay taxes,
for the authorities are God's servants,
who give their full time to governing.
Give everyone what you owe him:
If you owe taxes, pay taxes;
if revenue, then revenue;
if respect, then respect;
if honour, then honour.　　ROMANS 13:5–7

Our duty to God

I hate, I despise your religious feasts;
I cannot stand your assemblies.
Even though you bring me burnt offerings
and grain offerings,
I will not accept them.
Though you bring choice fellowship offerings,
I will have no regard for them.
Away with the noise of your songs!
I will not listen to the music of your harps.
But let justice roll on like a river,
righteousness like a never-failing stream!   AMOS 5:21–24

With what shall I come before the Lord
and bow down before the exalted God?
Shall I come before him with burnt offerings,
with calves a year old?
He has showed you, O man, what is good.
And what does the Lord require of you?
To act justly and to love mercy
and to walk humbly with your God.   MICAH 6:6,8

If anyone considers himself religious
and yet does not keep a tight rein on his tongue,
he deceives himself and his religion is worthless.
Religion that God our Father
     accepts as pure and faultless is this:
to look after orphans and widows in their distress
and to keep oneself from being polluted by the world.
     JAMES 1:26,27

God sees the truth

Jesus said to his disciples,
'Beware of the teachers of the law.
They like to walk round in flowing robes
and love to be greeted in the market-places
and have the most important seats in the synagogues
and the places of honour at banquets.
They devour widows' houses
and for a show make lengthy prayers.
Such men will be punished most severely.'
As he looked up, Jesus saw the rich
putting their gifts into the temple treasury.
He also saw a poor widow
put in two very small copper coins.
'I tell you the truth,' he said,
'this poor widow has put in more than all the others.
All these people gave their gifts out of their wealth;
but she out of her poverty
put in all she had to live on.'   LUKE 20:45 – 21:4

Now a man named Ananias,
together with his wife Sapphira,
also sold a piece of property.
With his wife's full knowledge
he kept back part of the money for himself,
but brought the rest and put it at the apostles' feet.
Then Peter said, 'Ananias, how is it
that Satan has so filled your heart
that you have lied to the Holy Spirit
and have kept for yourself some of the money
        you received for the land?
. . . You have not lied to men but to God.'
When Ananias heard this, he fell down and died.
And great fear seized all who heard what had happened.
                                    ACTS 5:1–3,4,5

Faith in action

What good is it, my brothers,
if a man claims to have faith but has no deeds?
Can such faith save him?
But someone will say,
'You have faith; I have deeds.'
Show me your faith without deeds,
and I will show you my faith by what I do.
As the body without the spirit is dead,
so faith without deeds is dead.   JAMES 2:14,18,26

We love because he first loved us.
If anyone says, 'I love God,'
yet hates his brother, he is a liar.
For anyone who does not love his brother,
whom he has seen,
cannot love God,
whom he has not seen.
And he has given us this command:
Whoever loves God
must also love his brother.   1 JOHN 4:19–21

I want you to stress these things,
so that those who have trusted in God
may be careful to devote themselves
     to doing what is good.
These things are excellent
and profitable for everyone.   TITUS 3:8

Our God is approachable

Praise awaits you, O God, in Zion;
to you our vows will be fulfilled.
O you who hear prayer,
to you all men will come.
When we were overwhelmed by sins,
you atoned for our transgressions.
Blessed is the man you choose
and bring near to live in your courts!
We are filled with the good things of your house,
     of your holy temple.   PSALM 65:1–4

This is the assurance we have
     in approaching God:
that if we ask anything according to his will,
he hears us.
And if we know that he hears us –
whatever we ask –
we know that we have what we asked of him.
                   1 JOHN 5:14,15

Let us then approach the throne of grace
     with confidence,
so that we may receive mercy
and find grace to help us
in our time of need.   HEBREWS 4:16

Worshipping in spirit and in truth

The rest of mankind
that were not killed by these plagues
still did not repent of the work of their hands;
they did not stop worshipping demons,
and idols of gold, silver,
bronze, stone and wood –
idols that cannot see or hear or walk.   REVELATION 9:20

Why do the nations say,
'Where is their God?'
Our God is in heaven;
he does whatever pleases him.
But their idols are silver and gold,
made by the hands of men.
They have mouths, but cannot speak,
eyes, but they cannot see;
they have ears, but cannot hear . . .
feet, but they cannot walk;
nor can they utter a sound with their throats.
Those who make them will be like them,
and so will all who trust in them.   PSALM 115:2–6,7,8

Jesus declared,
'. . . We worship what we do know,
for salvation is from the Jews.
Yet a time is coming and has now come
when the true worshippers will worship the Father
in spirit and truth,
for they are the kind of worshippers
     the Father seeks.
God is spirit,
and his worshippers must worship
in spirit and in truth.'   JOHN 4:22–24

Many and different contributions

Your procession has come into view, O God,
the procession of my God and King
    into the sanctuary.
In front are the singers,
after them the musicians;
with them are the maidens playing tambourines.
Praise God in the great congregation.   PSALM 68:24–26

As the offering began,
singing to the Lord began also,
accompanied by trumpets
and the instruments of David king of Israel.
The whole assembly bowed in worship. . .
So they sang praises with gladness
and bowed their heads and worshipped.

            2 CHRONICLES 29:27,28,30

Praise the Lord.
Praise God in his sanctuary;
praise him in his mighty heavens.
Praise him for his acts of power;
praise him for his surpassing greatness.
Praise him with the sounding of the trumpet,
praise him with the harp and lyre,
praise him with tambourine and dancing,
praise him with the strings and flute,
praise him with the clash of cymbals,
praise him with resounding cymbals.
Let everything that has breath praise the Lord.
Praise the Lord.

            PSALM 150:1–6

Worshipping together

Praise the Lord.
Praise the name of the Lord;
Praise him, you servants of the Lord,
you who minister in the house of the Lord,
in the courts of the house of our God.
Praise the Lord, for the Lord is good:
sing praise to his name, for that is pleasant.   PSALM 135:1–3

Speak to one another
with psalms, hymns and spiritual songs.
Sing and make music in your heart
to the Lord.   EPHESIANS 5:19

Be joyful always;
pray continually;
give thanks in all circumstances,
for this is God's will for you
in Christ Jesus.   1 THESSALONIANS 5:16–18

Then I heard every creature
in heaven and on earth
and under the earth and on the sea,
and all that is in them, singing:
'To him who sits on the throne and to the Lamb
be praise and honour and glory and power,
for ever and ever!'   REVELATION 5:13

Now we are all here in the presence of God
to listen to everything
the Lord has commanded you to tell us.   ACTS 10:33

Scripture, read and understood

Do not let this Book of the Law
    depart from your mouth;
meditate on it day and night,
so that you may be careful to do
    everything written in it.
Then you will be prosperous and successful.   JOSHUA 1:8.

Everyone who prophesies
speaks to men for their strengthening,
    encouragement and comfort. . .
He who prophesies
edifies the church.   1 CORINTHIANS 14:3,4

Ezra the priest
brought the Law before the assembly,
which was made up of men and women
and all who were able to understand.
He read it aloud from daybreak till noon . . .
and all the people listened attentively
to the Book of the Law.
Ezra the scribe
stood on a high wooden platform
built for the occasion. . .
He opened the book.
All the people could see him
    because he was standing above them;
and as he opened it, the people all stood up.
Ezra praised the Lord, the great God;
and all the people lifted their hands
    and responded, 'Amen! Amen!'
Then they bowed down and worshipped the Lord
with their faces to the ground.   NEHEMIAH 8:2,3,4,5,6

September 17th   The church's worship

Services, clear and comprehensible

So if the whole church comes together
and everyone speaks in tongues,
and some who do not understand
    or some unbelievers come in,
will they not say that you are out of your mind?
But if an unbeliever
    or someone who does not understand
comes in while everybody is prophesying,
he will be convinced by all that he is a sinner
and will be judged by all,
and the secrets of his heart will be laid bare.
So he will fall down and worship God, exclaiming,
'God is really among you!'   1 CORINTHIANS 14:23–25

The Levites read from the Book of the Law of God,
making it clear and giving the meaning
so that the people could understand
    what was being read.
Then all the people went away to eat and drink,
to send portions of food and to celebrate with great joy,
because they now understood the words
that had been made known to them.   NEHEMIAH 8:8,12

In the church
I would rather speak five intelligible words
to instruct others
than ten thousand words
in a tongue.   1 CORINTHIANS 14:19

Praise in music and song

It is good to praise the Lord
and make music to your name, O Most High,
to proclaim your love in the morning
and your faithfulness at night,
to the music of the ten-stringed lyre
and the melody of the harp.
For you make me glad by your deeds, O Lord;
I sing for joy at the work of your hands.   PSALM 92:1–4

In the days of David and Asaph,
there had been directors for the singers
and for the songs of praise
    and thanksgiving to God.
So in the days of Zerubbabel
and of Nehemiah,
all Israel contributed the daily portions
for the singers and gatekeepers.   NEHEMIAH 12:46,47

Sing to the Lord a new song;
sing to the Lord, all the earth.
Sing to the Lord, praise his name;
proclaim his salvation day after day.
Declare his glory among the nations,
his marvellous deeds among all peoples.
Splendour and majesty are before him;
strength and glory are in his sanctuary.
Ascribe to the Lord, O families of nations,
ascribe to the Lord glory and strength.   PSALM 96:1–3,6,7

Singing a new song

Your decrees are the theme of my song
wherever I lodge.
In the night I remember your name, O Lord,
and I will keep your law.
This has been my practice:
I obey your precepts.
You are my portion, O Lord;
I have promised to obey your words.   PSALM 119:54–57

Now the Spirit of the Lord
had departed from Saul,
and an evil spirit from the Lord
    tormented him.
Saul sent messengers to Jesse and said,
'Send me your son David,
    who is with the sheep.'
Whenever the spirit from God came upon Saul,
David would take his harp and play.
Then relief would come to Saul,
he would feel better,
and the evil spirit would leave him.   I SAMUEL 16:14,19,23

Sing to the Lord a new song,
for he has done marvellous things . . .
Shout for joy to the Lord, all the earth,
burst into jubilant song with music;
make music to the Lord with the harp,
with the harp and the sound of singing,
with trumpets and the blast of the ram's horn –
shout for joy before the Lord, the King.   PSALM 98:1,4–6

The breaking of bread

Jesus said to them,
'. . . Did not the Christ have to suffer these things
and then enter his glory?'
As they approached the village
        to which they were going,
Jesus acted as if he were going further.
But they urged him strongly,
'Stay with us, for it is nearly evening;
the day is almost over.'
So he went in to stay with them.
When he was at the table with them,
he took bread, gave thanks, broke it
and began to give it to them.
Then their eyes were opened
and they recognised him,
and he disappeared from their sight.   LUKE 24:25,26,28–31

Whenever you eat this bread and drink this cup,
you proclaim the Lord's death until he comes.
Therefore, whoever eats the bread
        or drinks the cup of the Lord
in an unworthy manner
will be guilty of sinning
against the body and blood of the Lord.
A man ought to examine himself
before he eats of the bread and drinks of the cup.
For anyone who eats and drinks
without recognising the body of the Lord
eats and drinks judgement on himself.

1 CORINTHIANS 11:26–29

The place of worship

But will God really dwell on earth?
The heavens, even the highest heaven,
  cannot contain you.
How much less this temple I have built!
Yet give attention to your servant's prayer
and his plea for mercy, O Lord my God . . .
May your eyes be open towards this temple
  night and day,
this place of which you said,
'My Name shall be there,'
so that you will hear the prayer your servant prays
  towards this place.
Hear the supplication of your servant
  and of your people Israel
when they pray towards this place.
Hear from heaven, your dwelling-place,
and when you hear, forgive.   1 KINGS 8:27,28,29,30

Praise the Lord, O my soul.
O Lord my God, you are very great;
you are clothed with splendour and majesty.
He wraps himself in light as with a garment;
he stretches out the heavens like a tent
and lays the beams of his upper chambers
  on their waters.   PSALM 104:1–3

Know that the Lord is God.
It is he who made us, and we are his;
we are his people, the sheep of his pasture.
Enter his gates with thanksgiving
and his courts with praise;
give thanks to him and praise his name.
For the Lord is good and his love endures for ever;
his faithfulness continues through all generations.
                                               PSALM 100:3–5

Misplaced confidence

This is the word that came to Jeremiah
    from the Lord:
'Stand at the gate of the Lord's house
and there proclaim this message . . .
"Reform your ways and your actions,
and I will let you live in this place.
Do not trust in deceptive words and say,
'This is the temple of the Lord,
the temple of the Lord, the temple of the Lord!'
Will you . . . then come and stand before me
in this house, which bears my Name,
and say, 'We are safe' –
safe to do all these detestable things?" '
JEREMIAH 7:1,2,3,4,9,10

Some of his disciples
were remarking about how the temple
    was adorned with beautiful stones
and with gifts dedicated to God.
But Jesus said,
'As for what you see here,
the time will come when not one stone
    will be left on another;
every one of them will be thrown down.'
LUKE 21:5,6

I did not see a temple in the city,
because the Lord God Almighty
and the Lamb
are its temple.
REVELATION 21:22

Not everyone who says to me, 'Lord, Lord,'
will enter the kingdom of heaven,
but only he who does the will of my Father
    who is in heaven.
MATTHEW 7:21

Worship and obey

Come, let us bow down in worship,
let us kneel before the Lord our Maker;
for he is our God
and we are the people of his pasture,
the flock under his care.
Today, if you hear his voice,
do not harden your hearts
as you did at Meribah.   PSALM 95:6–8

'As for you, son of man,
your countrymen are talking together about you
by the walls
and at the doors of the houses,
saying to each other,
"Come and hear
the message that has come from the Lord."
My people come to you, as they usually do,
and sit before you to listen to your words,
but they do not put them into practice.
With their mouths they express devotion,
but their hearts are greedy for unjust gain.
Indeed, to them you are nothing more
than one who sings love songs
     with a beautiful voice
and plays an instrument well,
for they hear your words
but do not put them into practice.
When all this comes true –
and it surely will –
then they will know
that a prophet has been among them.'   EZEKIEL 33:30–33

God's temple in us

How lovely is your dwelling-place,
O Lord Almighty!
My soul yearns, even faints
    for the courts of the Lord;
my heart and my flesh
cry out for the living God.
Blessed are those who dwell in your house;
they are ever praising you.
Blessed are those whose strength is in you.   PSALM 84:1,2,4,5

As you come to him, the living Stone –
rejected by men but chosen by God
    and precious to him –
you also, like living stones,
are being built into a spiritual house
to be a holy priesthood,
offering spiritual sacrifices acceptable to God
through Jesus Christ.   1 PETER 2:4,5

In him
the whole building is joined together
and rises to become a holy temple
in the Lord.
And in him
you too are being built together
to become a dwelling in which God lives
by his Spirit.   EPHESIANS 2:21,22

The presence of God

The man brought me to the gate facing east,
and I saw the glory of the God of Israel
coming from the east.
His voice was like the roar of rushing waters,
and the land was radiant with his glory.
I fell face down.
The glory of the Lord entered the temple
through the gate facing east.
Then the Spirit lifted me up
and brought me into the inner court,
and the glory ot the Lord
    filled the temple.   EZEKIEL 43:1,2,4,5

You are . . . God's building. . .
For no-one can lay any foundation
other than the one already laid,
which is Jesus Christ.
If any man builds on this foundation
using gold, silver, costly stones,
    wood, hay or straw,
his work will be shown for what it is,
because the Day will bring it to light.
It will be revealed with fire,
and the fire will test the quality
    of each man's work.
Don't you know
that you yourselves are God's temple
and that God's Spirit lives in you?
If anyone destroys God's temple,
God will destroy him;
for God's temple is sacred,
and you are that temple.   1 CORINTHIANS 3:9,11–13,16,17

God's call to sacrifice

Already you have all you want!
Already you have become rich!
You have become kings – and that without us!
How I wish that you really had become kings
so that we might be kings with you!
For it seems to me
that God has put us apostles on display
    at the end of the procession,
like men condemned to die in the arena.
We have been made a spectacle to the whole universe,
to angels as well as to men.
We are fools for Christ,
but you are so wise in Christ!
We are weak, but you are strong!
You are honoured, we are dishonoured!

                    1 CORINTHIANS 4:8–10

I know your deeds,
that you are neither cold nor hot.
I wish you were either one or the other!
So, because you are lukewarm – neither hot nor cold –
I am about to spit you out of my mouth.
You say, 'I am rich;
I have acquired wealth and do not need a thing.'
But you do not realise that you are wretched,
pitiful, poor, blind and naked.
I counsel you to buy from me gold refined in the fire,
so that you can become rich. . .   REVELATION 3:15–18

Generosity is fundamental

'All these I have kept since I was a boy,'
    he said.
When Jesus heard him, he said to him,
'You still lack one thing.
Sell everything you have and give to the poor,
and you will have treasure in heaven.
Then come, follow me.'
When he heard this, he became very sad,
because he was a man of great wealth.
Jesus looked at him and said,
'How hard it is
for the rich to enter the kingdom of God!'   LUKE 18:21–24

Command those who are rich in this present world
not to be arrogant nor to put their hope in wealth,
which is so uncertain,
but to put their hope in God,
who richly provides us with everything
    for our enjoyment.
Command them to do good,
to be rich in good deeds,
and to be generous and willing to share.
In this way they will lay up treasure for themselves
    as a firm foundation for the coming age,
so that they may take hold of the life
that is truly life.   1 TIMOTHY 6:17–19

Accepting sacrifice for Jesus' sake

The devil led him up to a high place
and showed him in an instant
    all the kingdoms of the world.
And he said to him,
'I will give you all their authority and splendour,
for it has been given to me,
and I can give it to anyone I want to.
So if you worship me, it will all be yours.'
Jesus answered,
'It is written: "Worship the Lord your God
and serve him only." '   LUKE 4:5–8

Then he called the crowd to him
    along with his disciples and said:
'If anyone would come after me,
he must deny himself
and take up his cross and follow me.
For whoever wants to save his life will lose it,
but whoever loses his life for me and for the gospel
will save it.
What good is it for a man to gain the whole world,
yet forfeit his soul?
Or what can a man give
in exchange for his soul?'   MARK 8:34–37

But whatever was to my profit
I now consider loss for the sake of Christ.   PHILIPPIANS 3:7

A right attitude to wealth

All the believers were one in heart and mind.
No-one claimed that any of his possessions
    was his own,
but they shared everything they had.
With great power
the apostles continued to testify
    to the resurrection of the Lord Jesus,
and much grace was with them all.
There were no needy persons among them.
For from time to time
those who owned lands or houses sold them,
brought the money from the sales
and put it at the apostles' feet,
and it was distributed to anyone
    as he had need.   ACTS 4:32–35

The older brother answered his father,
'Look! All these years I've been slaving for you
and never disobeyed your orders.
Yet you never gave me even a young goat
so I could celebrate with my friends.
But when this son of yours
who has squandered your property with prostitutes
    comes home,
you kill the fattened calf for him!'
'My son,' the father said,
'you are always with me,
and everything I have is yours.'   LUKE 15:29–31

Then Jesus said to them,
'Watch out!
Be on your guard against all kinds of greed;
a man's life does not consist
    in the abundance of his possessions.'   LUKE 12:15

Giving in accordance with what you have

Jesus sat down
opposite the place where the offerings were put
and watched the crowd putting their money
    into the temple treasury.
Many rich people threw in large amounts.
But a poor widow came
and put in two very small copper coins
    worth only a fraction of a penny.
Calling his disciples to him, Jesus said,
'I tell you the truth,
this poor widow has put more into the treasury
    than all the others.
They all gave out of their wealth;
but she, out of her poverty, put in everything –
all she had to live on.'
    MARK 12:41–44

Last year you were the first not only to give
but also to have the desire to do so.
Now finish the work,
so that your eager willingness to do it
may be matched by your completion of it,
according to your means.
For if the willingness is there,
the gift is acceptable according to what one has,
not according to what he does not have.
    2 CORINTHIANS 8:10–12

Devoting our resources to God

Everyone who was willing
and whose heart moved him
came and brought an offering to the Lord
for the work on the Tent of Meeting,
for all its services, and for the sacred garments.
Every skilled woman spun with her hands
and brought what she had spun –
blue, purple or scarlet yarn or fine linen.
And all the women who were willing and had the skill
    spun the goat hair.
The leaders brought onyx stones and other gems
to be mounted on the ephod and breastpiece.
They also brought spices and olive oil
for the light and for the anointing oil
and for the fragrant incense.
All the Israelite men and women who were willing
brought to the Lord freewill offerings
for all the work
the Lord through Moses
had commanded them to do.   EXODUS 35:21,25–29

Wealth and honour come from you;
you are the ruler of all things.
In your hands are strength and power
to exalt and give strength to all.
Now, our God, we give you thanks,
and praise your glorious name.
'But who am I, and who are my people,
that we should be able to give as generously as this?
Everything comes from you,
and we have given you
only what comes from your hand.'   1 CHRONICLES 29:12–14

Honouring God by giving

Then the word of the Lord
came through the prophet Haggai:
'Is it a time for you yourselves
to be living in your panelled houses,
while this house remains a ruin?
You have planted much, but have harvested little.
You eat, but never have enough.
You drink, but never have your fill.
You put on clothes, but are not warm.
You earn wages, only to put them in a purse
    with holes in it.
Go up into the mountains and bring down timber
    and build the house,
so that I may take pleasure in it
    and be honoured,' says the Lord.
'You expected much, but see, it turned out to be little.
What you brought home, I blew away.
Why?' declares the Lord Almighty.
'Because of my house, which remains a ruin,
while each of you is busy with his own house.'

HAGGAI 1:3,4,6,8,9

'Will a man rob God? Yet you rob me.
But you ask, "How do we rob you?"
In tithes and offerings.
You are under a curse – the whole nation of you –
because you are robbing me.
Bring the whole tithe into the storehouse,
that there may be food in my house.
Test me in this,' says the Lord Almighty,
'and see if I will not throw open
    the floodgates of heaven
and pour out so much blessing
that you will not have room enough for it.' MALACHI 3:8–10

Giving to other parts of the church

On the first day of every week,
each one of you should set aside a sum of money
    in keeping with his income,
saving it up, so that when I come
no collections will have to be made.
Then, when I arrive,
I will give letters of introduction
    to the men you approve
and send them with your gift to Jerusalem.
If it seems advisable for me to go also,
they will accompany me.   1 CORINTHIANS 16:2–4

Our desire is not that others might be relieved
while you are hard pressed,
but that there might be equality.
At the present time
your plenty will supply what they need,
so that in turn
their plenty will supply what you need.
Then there will be equality,
as it is written:
'He that gathered much did not have too much,
 and he that gathered little did not have too little.'
    2 CORINTHIANS 8:13–15

The promise of joy at harvest

Be not afraid, O land; be glad and rejoice.
Surely the Lord has done great things.
Be not afraid, O wild animals,
for the open pastures are becoming green.
The trees are bearing their fruit;
the fig-tree and the vine yield their riches.
Be glad, O people of Zion,
rejoice in the Lord your God,
for he has given you a teacher for righteousness.
He sends you abundant showers,
both autumn and spring rains, as before.
The threshing-floors will be filled with grain;
the vats will overflow with new wine and oil.
You will have plenty to eat, until you are full,
and you will praise the name of the Lord your God,
who has worked wonders for you;
never again will my people be shamed.   JOEL 2:21–24,26

Those who sow in tears
will reap with songs of joy.
He who goes out weeping,
carrying seed to sow,
will return with songs of joy,
carrying sheaves with him.   PSALM 126:5,6

Why we should give thanks

Count off seven weeks
from the time you begin to put the sickle
    to the standing corn.
Then celebrate the Feast of Weeks to the Lord your
    God. . .
For seven days celebrate the Feast to the Lord your God
at the place the Lord will choose.
For the Lord your God will bless you in all your harvest
and in all the work of your hands,
and your joy will be complete.
Each of you must bring a gift
    in proportion to the way the Lord your God
    has blessed you.   DEUTERONOMY 16:9,10,15,17

Take some of the first fruits
of all that you produce from the soil of the land
    that the Lord your God is giving you
and put them in a basket.
Then go to the place that the Lord your God
    will choose as a dwelling for his Name.
Then you shall declare before the Lord your God:
'We cried out to the Lord, the God of our fathers,
and the Lord heard our voice
and saw our misery, toil and oppression.
He brought us to this place and gave us this land,
a land flowing with milk and honey;
and now I bring the firstfruits of the soil
    that you, O Lord, have given me.'
Place the basket before the Lord your God
and bow down before him.
And you and the Levites and the aliens among you
shall rejoice in all the good things
the Lord your God has given to you
    and your household.   DEUTERONOMY 26:2,5,7,9–11

The people of God

You are a chosen people, a royal priesthood,
a holy nation, a people belonging to God,
that you may declare
the praises of him who called you out of darkness
into his wonderful light.
Once you were not a people,
but now you are the people of God;
once you had not received mercy,
but now you have received mercy.　　　　1 PETER 2:9,10

In the place where it was said to them,
'You are not my people,'
they will be called 'sons of the living God.'
I will betroth you to me for ever;
I will betroth you in righteousness and justice,
in love and compassion.
I will betroth you in faithfulness,
and you will acknowledge the Lord.　　　HOSEA 1:10, 2:19,20

I heard a loud voice from the throne saying,
'Now the dwelling of God is with men,
and he will live with them.
They will be his people,
and God himself will be with them
and be their God.
He will wipe every tear from their eyes.
There will be no more death or mourning
or crying or pain,
for the old order of things
has passed away.'　　　　　REVELATION 21:3,4

Fellowship in Christ

As for the saints who are in the land,
they are the glorious ones in whom is all my delight.

PSALM 16:3

They devoted themselves to the apostles' teaching
and to the fellowship,
to the breaking of bread and to prayer.
All the believers were together
and had everything in common.
Selling their possessions and goods,
they gave to anyone as he had need.
Every day
they continued to meet together in the temple courts.
They broke bread in their homes
and ate together with glad and sincere hearts,
praising God
and enjoying the favour of all the people.
And the Lord added to their number daily
those who were being saved.

ACTS 2:42,44–47

Let us consider how we may spur one another on
towards love and good deeds.
Let us not give up meeting together,
as some are in the habit of doing,
but let us encourage one another –
and all the more
as you see the Day approaching.

HEBREWS 10:24,25

The debt to love one another

Let no debt remain outstanding,
except the continuing debt to love one another,
for he who loves his fellow man
has fulfilled the law.
The commandments,
'Do not commit adultery,'
'Do not murder,'
'Do not steal,'
'Do not covet,'
and whatever other commandments there may be,
are summed up in this one rule:
'Love your neighbour as yourself.'
Love does no harm to its neighbour.
Therefore love is the fulfilment of the law.   ROMANS 13:8–10

We love because he first loved us.
If anyone says, 'I love God,' yet hates his brother,
he is a liar.
For anyone who does not love his brother,
whom he has seen,
cannot love God,
whom he has not seen.
And he has given us this command:
Whoever loves God
must also love his brother.   1 JOHN 4:19–21

Love for each other

'My children,
I will be with you only a little longer. . .
A new commandment I give you:
Love one another.
As I have loved you, so you must love one another.
All men will know that you are my disciples
if you love one another.'   JOHN 13:33,34,35

Dear friends, let us love one another,
for love comes from God.
Everyone who loves
has been born of God and knows God.
Whoever does not love does not know God,
because God is love.   1 JOHN 4:7,8

Now that you have purified yourselves
by obeying the truth
so that you have sincere love for your brothers,
love one another deeply, from the heart.
For you have been born again,
not of perishable seed, but of imperishable,
through the living and enduring word of God.   1 PETER 1:22,23

I am not writing you a new command
but one we have had from the beginning.
I ask that we love one another.
And this is love:
that we walk in obedience to his commands.
As you have heard from the beginning,
his command is that you walk in love.   2 JOHN 5,6

Brothers and sisters in the Lord

Someone told Jesus,
'Your mother and brothers are standing outside,
wanting to speak to you.'
He replied,
'Who is my mother, and who are my brothers?'
Pointing to his disciples, he said,
'Here are my mother and my brothers.
For whoever does the will of my Father in heaven
is my brother and sister and mother.' MATTHEW 12:47–50

And now, dear children, continue in him,
so that when he appears
we may be confident
and unashamed before him at his coming.
If you know that he is righteous,
you know that everyone who does what is right
has been born of him.
How great is the love the Father has lavished on us,
that we should be called children of God!
And that is what we are!
The reason the world does not know us
is that it did not know him.
Dear friends, now we are children of God,
and what we will be has not yet been made known.
But we know that when he appears,
we shall be like him,
for we shall see him as he is. 1 JOHN 2:28–3:2

Adopted as sons

Praise be to the God and Father
of our Lord Jesus Christ,
who has blessed us in the heavenly realms
with every spiritual blessing in Christ.
For he chose us in him
before the creation of the world
to be holy and blameless in his sight.
In love he predestined us
to be adopted as his sons through Jesus Christ,
in accordance with his pleasure and will.   EPHESIANS 1:3–5

For those God foreknew
he also predestined
to be conformed to the likeness of his Son,
that he might be the firstborn among many brothers.
                                          ROMANS 8:29

Those who are led by the Spirit of God
are sons of God.
For you did not receive a spirit
that makes you a slave again to fear,
but you received the Spirit of sonship.
And by him we cry, '*Abba*, Father.'
The Spirit himself testifies with our spirit
that we are God's children.
Now if we are children, then we are heirs –
heirs of God and co-heirs with Christ,
if indeed we share in his sufferings
in order that we may also share in his glory.   ROMANS 8:14–17

Be united!

I appeal to you, brothers,
in the name of our Lord Jesus Christ,
that all of you agree with one another
so that there may be no divisions among you
and that you may be perfectly united
in mind and thought.
My brothers, some from Chloe's household
have informed me that there are quarrels among you.
What I mean is this:
One of you says, 'I follow Paul';
another, 'I follow Apollos';
another, 'I follow Cephas';
still another, 'I follow Christ.'
Is Christ divided?
Was Paul crucified for you?
Were you baptised into the name of Paul?

1 CORINTHIANS 1:10–13

Have we not all one Father?
Did not one God create us?
Why do we profane the covenant of our fathers
by breaking faith with one another?   MALACHI 2:10

How good and pleasant it is
when brothers live together in unity!
It is like precious oil poured on the head,
running down on the beard,
running down on Aaron's beard,
down upon the collar of his robes.
It is as if the dew of Hermon
were falling on Mount Zion.
For there the Lord bestows his blessing,
even life for evermore.   PSALM 133

Receive the word of God

Jesus said, 'This is what the kingdom of God is like.
A man scatters seed on the ground.
All by itself the soil produces corn –
first the stalk, then the ear,
then the full kernel in the ear.'   MARK 4:26,28

What, after all, is Apollos?
And what is Paul?
Only servants, through whom you came to believe –
as the Lord has assigned to each his task.
I planted the seed,
Apollos watered it,
but God made it grow.
The man who plants and the man who waters
have one purpose,
and each will be rewarded according to his own labour.
For we are God's fellow-workers;
you are God's field, God's building.   1 CORINTHIANS 3:5,6,8,9

We thank God because we have heard of your faith in
     Christ Jesus
and of the love you have for all the saints –
the faith and love that spring
from the hope that is stored up for you in heaven,
and that you have already heard about
in the word of truth,
the gospel that has come to you.
All over the world
this gospel is producing fruit and growing,
just as it has been doing among you
since the day you heard it
and understood God's grace in all its truth.   COLOSSIANS 1:4–6

Be slow to fault each other

Who can discern his errors?
Forgive my hidden faults.
May the words of my mouth
and the meditation of my heart
be pleasing in your sight,
O Lord, my Rock and my Redeemer.   PSALM 19:12,14

Jesus told them this parable:
'Can a blind man lead a blind man?
Will they not both fall into a pit?
A student is not above his teacher,
but everyone who is fully trained
will be like his teacher.
Why do you look at the speck of sawdust
in your brother's eye
and pay no attention to the plank
in your own eye?
You hypocrite,
first take the plank out of your eye,
and then you will see clearly
to remove the speck from your brother's eye.'
                                        LUKE 6:39–41,42

Brothers, do not slander one another.
Anyone who speaks against his brother or judges him,
speaks against the law and judges it.
When you judge the law, you are not keeping it,
but sitting in judgement on it.
There is only one Law-giver and Judge,
the one who is able to save and destroy.
But you – who are you to judge your neighbour?
                                        JAMES 4:11,12

Do not pass judgement!

You speak continually against your brother
and slander your own mother's son.
These things you have done and I kept silent;
you thought I was altogether like you.
But I will rebuke you and accuse you to your face.
Consider this, you who forget God,
or I will tear you to pieces, with none to rescue:
He who sacrifices thank-offerings honours me,
and he prepares the way
so that I may show him the salvation of God.

PSALM 50:20–23

You, therefore, have no excuse,
you who pass judgement on someone else,
for at whatever point you judge the other,
you are condemning yourself,
because you who pass judgement do the same things.
Now we know
that God's judgement against those who do such things
is based on truth.
So when you, a mere man,
pass judgement on them and yet do the same things,
do you think you will escape God's judgement?
Or do you show contempt
for the riches of his kindness, tolerance and patience,
not realising that God's kindness
leads you towards repentance?

ROMANS 2:1–4

Do not condemn, but support

The teachers of the law and the Pharisees said to Jesus,
    'Teacher,
this woman was caught in the act of adultery.
In the Law
Moses commanded us to stone such women.
Now what do you say?'
Jesus bent down and started to write on the ground
with his finger.
When they kept on questioning him,
he straightened up and said to them,
'If any one of you is without sin,
let him be the first to throw a stone at her.'
At this, those who heard
    began to go away one at a time,
the older ones first,
until only Jesus was left,
with the woman still standing there.
Jesus straightened up and asked her,
'Woman, where are they? Has no-one condemned you?'
'No-one sir,' she said.
'Then neither do I condemn you,' Jesus declared.
'Go now and leave your life of sin.'   JOHN 8:4,5,6,7,9–11

Brothers,
if someone is caught in a sin,
you who are spiritual should restore him gently.
But watch yourself,
or you also may be tempted.
Carry each other's burdens,
and in this way you will fulfil
    the law of Christ.   GALATIANS 6:1,2

The importance of example

Be careful . . . that the exercise of your freedom
does not become a stumbling block to the weak.
For if anyone with a weak conscience
sees you who have this knowledge
　　　eating in an idol's temple,
won't he be emboldened to eat
　　　what has been sacrificed to idols?
So this weak brother, for whom Christ died,
is destroyed by your knowledge.
When you sin against your brothers in this way
and wound their weak conscience,
you sin against Christ.　　　　　　　1 CORINTHIANS 8:9–12

Make up your mind
　　　not to put any stumbling-block or obstacle
　　　in your brother's way.
If your brother is distressed because of what you eat,
you are no longer acting in love.
Do not by your eating
destroy your brother for whom Christ died.
Let us therefore make every effort
　　　to do what leads to peace
　　　and to mutual edification.　　　　ROMANS 14:13,15,19

None of us lives to himself alone
and none of us dies to himself alone.
If we live, we live to the Lord;
and if we die, we die to the Lord.
So, whether we live or die,
we belong to the Lord.
So then, each of us will give an account of himself
　　　to God.
Therefore let us stop passing judgement on one another.
　　　　　　　　　　　　　　　　ROMANS 14:7,8,12,13

Arguments offend and cause pain

Teach me, and I will be quiet;
show me where I have been wrong.
How painful are honest words!
But what do your arguments prove?
Do you mean to correct what I say,
and treat the words of a despairing man as wind?
But now be so kind as to look at me.
Would I lie to your face?
Relent, do not be unjust;
reconsider, for my integrity is at stake.
Is there any wickedness on my lips?
Can my mouth not discern malice? JOB 6:24–26,28–30

Keep reminding them of these things.
Warn them before God
against quarrelling about words;
it is of no value,
and only ruins those who listen. 2 TIMOTHY 2:14

Accept him whose faith is weak,
without passing judgement on disputable matters.
Who are you to judge someone else's servant?
To his own master he stands or falls.
And he will stand,
for the Lord is able to make him stand. ROMANS 14:1,4

Let love conquer pride!

Timothy, guard what has been entrusted to your care.
Turn away from godless chatter
and the opposing ideas
    of what is falsely called knowledge,
which some have professed
and in so doing have wandered from the faith.

1 TIMOTHY 6:20,21

We know that we all possess knowledge.
Knowledge puffs up, but love builds up.
The man who thinks he knows something
does not yet know as he ought to know.
But the man who loves God is known by God.

1 CORINTHIANS 8:1,2,3

They said to each other,
'Come, let's make bricks and bake them thoroughly.'
They used brick instead of stone,
and tar instead of mortar.
Then they said, 'Come, let us build ourselves a city,
with a tower that reaches to the heavens,
so that we may make a name for ourselves
and not be scattered over the face of the whole earth.'
But the Lord came down to see the city
and the tower that the men were building.
The Lord said, 'If as one people
speaking the same language
they have begun to do this,
then nothing they plan to do
will be impossible for them.
Come, let us go down and confuse their language
so they will not understand each other.'
So the Lord scattered them from there
over all the earth,
and they stopped building the city.

GENESIS 11:3–8

A warning to all believers

It is impossible
> for those who have once been enlightened,
who have tasted the heavenly gift,
who have shared in the Holy Spirit,
who have tasted the goodness of the word of God
and the powers of the coming age,
if they fall away,
to be brought back to repentance,
because to their loss
they are crucifying the Son of God all over again
and subjecting him to public disgrace.   HEBREWS 6:4–6

I know your deeds;
you have a reputation of being alive,
but you are dead.
Wake up!
Strengthen what remains, and is about to die,
for I have not found your deeds complete
> in the sight of my God.
Remember, therefore, what you have received and heard;
obey it, and repent.
But if you do not wake up, I will come like a thief,
and you will not know at what time I will come to you.
Yet you have a few people in Sardis
> who have not soiled their clothes.
They will walk with me dressed in white,
for they are worthy.
He who overcomes will, like them, be dressed in white.
I will never erase his name from the book of life,
but will acknowledge his name before my Father
> and his angels.   REVELATION 3:1–5

God's gifts to the church

There are different kinds of gifts,
but the same Spirit.
There are different kinds of service,
but the same Lord.
There are different kinds of working,
but the same God works all of them in all men.
Now to each one the manifestation of the Spirit is given
for the common good.　　　1 CORINTHIANS 12:4–7

We have different gifts,
according to the grace given us.
If a man's gift is prophesying,
let him use it in proportion to his faith.
If it is serving, let him serve;
if it is teaching, let him teach;
if it is encouraging, let him encourage;
if it is contributing to the needs of others,
　　let him give generously;
if it is leadership, let him govern diligently;
if it is showing mercy, let him do it cheerfully.
　　　　　ROMANS 12:6–8

Each one should use whatever gift he has received
to serve others,
faithfully administering God's grace
　　in its various forms.
If anyone speaks,
he should do it as one speaking the very words of God.
If anyone serves,
he should do it with the strength God provides,
so that in all things God may be praised
　　through Jesus Christ.
To him be the glory and the power
for ever and ever. Amen.　　　1 PETER 4:10,11

The gifts are complementary

Just as each of us has one body with many members,
and these members do not all have the same function,
so in Christ we who are many form one body,
and each member belongs to all the others.   ROMANS 12:4,5

God has combined the members of the body
and has given greater honour
to the parts that lacked it,
so that there should be no division in the body,
but that its parts should have equal concern
for each other.
If one part suffers, every part suffers with it;
if one part is honoured,
every part rejoices with it.
Now you are the body of Christ,
and each one of you is part of it.   1 CORINTHIANS 12:24–27

To each one of us
grace has been given
as Christ apportioned it.
It was he who gave some to be apostles,
some to be prophets, some to be evangelists,
and some to be pastors and teachers,
to prepare God's people for works of service,
so that the body of Christ may be built up
until we all reach unity in the faith
and in the knowledge of the Son of God
and become mature,
attaining to the whole measure
of the fulness of Christ.
From him the whole body,
joined and held together by every supporting ligament,
grows and builds itself up in love,
as each part does its work.   EPHESIANS 4:7,11–13,16

The most important gift

If I speak in the tongues of men and of angels,
but have not love,
I am only a resounding gong
or a clanging cymbal.
If I have the gift of prophecy
and can fathom all mysteries and all knowledge,
and if I have a faith that can move mountains,
but have not love,
I am nothing.
If I give all I possess to the poor
and surrender my body to the flames,
but have not love,
I gain nothing.
Love is patient, love is kind.
It does not envy, it does not boast,
it is not proud.
It is not rude, it is not self-seeking,
it is not easily angered,
it keeps no record of wrongs.
Love does not delight in evil
but rejoices with the truth.
It always protects, always trusts,
always hopes, always perseveres.
Love never fails.
But where there are prophecies, they will cease;
where there are tongues, they will be stilled;
where there is knowledge, it will pass away.
For we know in part
and we prophesy in part,
but when perfection comes, the imperfect disappears.

1 CORINTHIANS 13:1–10

Speak to be helpful

Therefore each of you must put off falsehood
and speak truthfully to his neighbour,
for we are all members of one body.
Do not let any unwholesome talk come out of your
    mouths,
but only what is helpful for building others up
according to their needs,
that it may benefit those who listen.
And do not grieve the Holy Spirit of God,
with whom you were sealed for the day of redemption.
Get rid of all bitterness, rage and anger,
brawling and slander,
along with every form of malice.
Be kind and compassionate to one another,
forgiving each other,
just as in Christ God forgave you.   EPHESIANS 4:25,29–32

The tongue is a small part of the body,
but it makes great boasts.
Consider what a great forest is set on fire
by a small spark.
The tongue also is a fire. . .   JAMES 3:5,6

O Lord, I call to you; come quickly to me.
Hear my voice when I call to you.
May my prayer be set before you like incense;
may the lifting up of my hands
be like the evening sacrifice.
Set a guard over my mouth, O Lord;
keep watch over the door of my lips.
Let not my heart be drawn to what is evil,
to take part in wicked deeds
with men who are evildoers;
let me not eat of their delicacies.   PSALM 141:1–4

Witness to faith

You are the light of the world.
A city on a hill cannot be hidden.
Neither do people light a lamp
and put it under a bowl.
Instead they put it on its stand,
and it gives light to everyone in the house.
In the same way,
let your light shine before men,
that they may see your good deeds
and praise your Father in heaven.   MATTHEW 5:14–16

Arise, shine, for your light has come,
and the glory of the Lord rises upon you.
See, darkness covers the earth
and thick darkness is over the peoples,
but the Lord rises upon you
and his glory appears over you.
Nations will come to your light,
and kings to the brightness of your dawn.   ISAIAH 60:1–3

For you were once darkness,
but now you are light in the Lord.
Live as children of light
(for the fruit of the light
consists in all goodness, righteousness and truth)
and find out what pleases the Lord.   EPHESIANS 5:8–10

The church family – in harmony

Therefore, as God's chosen people,
holy and dearly loved,
clothe yourselves with compassion, kindness,
humility, gentleness and patience.
Bear with each other
and forgive whatever grievances you may have
    against one another.
Forgive as the Lord forgave you.
And over all these virtues put on love,
which binds them all together in perfect unity.
Let the peace of Christ rule in your hearts,
since as members of one body
    you were called to peace.
And be thankful.
Let the word of Christ dwell in you richly
as you teach and admonish one another with all wisdom,
and as you sing psalms, hymns and spiritual songs
with gratitude in your hearts to God.   COLOSSIANS 3:12–16

Rejoice in the Lord always.
I will say it again: Rejoice!
Let your gentleness be evident to all.
The Lord is near.
Do not be anxious about anything,
but in everything, by prayer and petition,
with thanksgiving,
present your requests to God.
And the peace of God,
which transcends all understanding,
will guard your hearts and your minds
in Christ Jesus.   PHILIPPIANS 4:4–7

The church family – in suffering

Give ear, O God, and hear;
open your eyes and see the desolation
of the city that bears your name.
We do not make requests of you
because we are righteous,
but because of your great mercy.
O Lord, listen! O Lord, forgive!
O Lord, hear and act!
For your sake, O my God, do not delay,
because your city and your people bear your name.

DANIEL 9:18,19

By the rivers of Babylon we sat and wept
when we remembered Zion.
For there our captors asked us for songs,
our tormentors demanded songs of joy;
they said, 'Sing us one of the songs of Zion!'
How can we sing the songs of the Lord
while in a foreign land?
If I forget you, O Jerusalem,
may my right hand forget its skill.

PSALM 137:1,3–5

I saw the Holy City, the new Jerusalem,
coming down out of heaven from God,
prepared as a bride
beautifully dressed for her husband.
And I heard a loud voice from the throne saying,
'Now the dwelling of God is with men,
and he will live with them.
They will be his people,
and God himself will be with them and be their God.
He will wipe every tear from their eyes.'

REVELATION 21:2–4

Two loyalties

'Why are you trying to trap me?' Jesus asked.
'Bring me a denarius and let me look at it.'
They brought the coin, and he asked them,
'Whose portrait is this?
And whose inscription?'
'Caesar's,' they replied.
Then Jesus said to them,
'Give to Caesar what is Caesar's
and to God what is God's.'   MARK 12:15–17

Submit yourselves for the Lord's sake
to every authority instituted among men:
whether to the king, as the supreme authority,
or to governors,
who are sent by him to punish those who do wrong
and to commend those who do right.
For it is God's will that by doing good
you should silence the ignorant talk of foolish men.
Live as free men, but do not use your freedom
as a cover-up for evil;
live as servants of God.
Show proper respect to everyone:
Love the brotherhood of believers,
fear God, honour the king.   1 PETER 2:13–17

Remind the people
to be subject to rulers and authorities,
to be obedient,
to be ready to do whatever is good,
to slander no-one,
to be peaceable and considerate,
and to show true humility towards all men.   TITUS 3:1,2

Supporting our leaders

Now we ask you, brothers,
to respect those who work hard among you,
who are over you in the Lord
and who admonish you.
Hold them in the highest regard in love
because of their work. . .

1 THESSALONIANS 5:12,13

One day Elisha went to Shunem.
And a well-to-do woman was there,
who urged him to stay for a meal.
So whenever he came by, he stopped there to eat.
She said to her husband,
'I know that this man who often comes our way
is a holy man of God.
Let's make a small room on the roof
and put in it a bed and a table,
a chair and a lamp for him.
Then he can stay there whenever he comes to us.'

2 KINGS 4:8–10

Who serves as a soldier
at his own expense?
Who plants a vineyard
and does not eat of its grapes?
Who tends a flock
and does not drink of the milk?
When the ploughman ploughs, and the thresher threshes,
they ought to do so
in the hope of sharing in the harvest.
If we have sown spiritual seed among you,
is it too much
if we reap a material harvest from you?

1 CORINTHIANS 9:7,10,11

Our responsibility towards leaders

At that time I said to you,
'You are too heavy a burden for me to carry alone.
How can I bear your problems and your burdens
and your disputes all by myself?
Choose some wise, understanding and respected men
from each of your tribes,
and I will set them over you.'
You answered me,
'What you propose to do is good.'
So I took the leading men of your tribes,
wise and respected men,
and appointed them to have authority over you. . .

DEUTERONOMY 1:9,12–15

Obey your leaders and submit to their authority.
They keep watch over you
as men who must give an account.
Obey them so that their work will be a joy,
not a burden,
for that would be of no advantage to you.
Pray for us.
We are sure that we have a clear conscience
and desire to live honourably in every way.

HEBREWS 13:17,18

Anyone who receives instruction in the word
must share all good things with his instructor.   GALATIANS 6:6

Church helpers

The Twelve
gathered all the disciples together and said,
'It would not be right for us
to neglect the ministry of the word of God
in order to wait on tables.
Brothers, choose seven men from among you
who are known to be full of the Spirit and wisdom.
We will turn this responsibility over to them
and will give our attention to prayer
and the ministry of the word.'   ACTS 6:2–4

Deacons, likewise, are to be men worthy of respect,
sincere, not indulging in much wine,
and not pursuing dishonest gain.
They must keep hold of the deep truths of the faith
with a clear conscience.
They must first be tested;
and then if there is nothing against them,
let them serve as deacons.
In the same way,
their wives are to be women worthy of respect,
not malicious talkers
but temperate and trustworthy in everything.
A deacon must be the husband of but one wife
and must manage his children and his household well.
Those who have served well
gain an excellent standing
and great assurance in their faith
in Christ Jesus.   1 TIMOTHY 3:8–13

November 1st   The church's leadership

The leader – character

The servant replied, 'Look,
in this town there is a man of God;
he is highly respected,
and everything he says comes true.
Let's go there now.
Perhaps he will tell us which way to take.'   1 SAMUEL 9:6

Now the overseer must be above reproach,
the husband of but one wife,
temperate, self-controlled,
respectable, hospitable,
able to teach, not given to much wine,
not violent but gentle,
not quarrelsome, not a lover of money.
He must manage his own family well
and see that his children obey him
with proper respect.
(If anyone does not know how to manage his own family,
how can he take care of God's church?)
He must not be a recent convert,
or he may become conceited
and fall under the same judgement as the devil.
He must also have a good reputation with outsiders. . .
    1 TIMOTHY 3:2–7

Since an overseer is entrusted with God's work,
he must be blameless – not overbearing,
not quick-tempered, not given to much wine,
not violent, not pursuing dishonest gain.
Rather he must be hospitable,
one who loves what is good,
who is self-controlled,
upright, holy and disciplined.   TITUS 1:7,8

The leader – maturity

Then King Rehoboam consulted the elders
who had served his father Solomon during his lifetime.
'How would you advise me to answer these people?'
he asked.
They replied,
'If today you will be a servant to these people
and serve them
and give them a favourable answer,
they will always be your servants.'
But Rehoboam rejected the advice the elders gave him
and consulted the young men
who had grown up with him
and were serving him.
The king answered the people harshly.
Rejecting the advice given him by the elders,
he followed the advice of the young men and said,
'My father made your yoke heavy;
I will make it even heavier.
My father scourged you with whips;
I will scourge you with scorpions.'   1 KINGS 12:6–8,13,14

Teach the older men to be temperate,
worthy of respect, self-controlled,
and sound in faith, in love and in endurance.
Similarly, encourage the young men to be self-controlled.
In everything set them an example
by doing what is good.
In your teaching show integrity, seriousness
and soundness of speech
that cannot be condemned,
so that those who oppose you
may be ashamed
because they have nothing bad to say about us.

                                                    TITUS 2:2,6–8

The leader – pastoral care

To the elders among you,
I appeal as a fellow elder. . .
Be shepherds of God's flock that is under your care,
serving as overseers –
not because you must, but because you are willing,
as God wants you to be;
not greedy for money, but eager to serve;
not lording it over those entrusted to you,
but being examples to the flock.   1 PETER 5:1,2,3

Because my flock lacks a shepherd
and so has been plundered
and has become food for all the wild animals,
and because my shepherds did not search for my flock
but cared for themselves rather than for my flock,
therefore, O shepherds,
hear the word of the Lord:
This is what the Sovereign Lord says:
I am against the shepherds
and will hold them accountable for my flock. . .
                                        EZEKIEL 34:8–10

Guard yourselves and all the flock
of which the Holy Spirit has made your overseers.
Be shepherds of the church of God,
which he bought with his own blood.   ACTS 20:28

Peter was hurt
because Jesus asked him the third time,
'Do you love me?'
He said, 'Lord, you know all things;
you know that I love you.'
Jesus said, 'Feed my sheep.'   JOHN 21:17

The leader and Scripture

Be careful to obey all the law
my servant Moses gave you;
do not turn from it to the right or to the left,
that you may be successful wherever you go.
Do not let this Book of the Law depart
    from your mouth;
meditate on it day and night,
so that you may be careful to do
    everything written in it.
Then you will be prosperous and successful.   JOSHUA 1:7,8

If you point these things out to the brothers,
you will be a good minister of Christ Jesus,
brought up in the truths of the faith
    and of the good teaching that you have followed.
Until I come,
devote yourself to the public reading of Scripture,
to preaching and to teaching.   1 TIMOTHY 4:6,13

Praise be to you, O Lord;
teach me your decrees.
With my lips I recount
all the laws that come from your mouth.
I rejoice in following your statutes
as one rejoices in great riches.
I meditate on your precepts and consider your ways.
I delight in your decrees;
I will not neglect your word.
Do good to your servant, and I will live;
I will obey your word.
Open my eyes
that I may see wonderful things in your law.

PSALM 119:12–18

Leading others to the Scriptures

So Moses wrote down this law
and gave it to the priests, the sons of Levi,
who carried the ark of the covenant of the Lord,
and to all the elders of Israel.
Then Moses commanded them. . .
'When all Israel comes to appear before
     the Lord your God
at the place he will choose,
you shall read this law before them in their hearing.
Assemble the people –
men, women and children,
and the aliens living in your towns –
so that they can listen
and learn to fear the Lord your God
and follow carefully all the words of this law.'

                  DEUTERONOMY 31:9,10,11,12

You then, my son,
be strong in the grace that is in Christ Jesus.
And the things you have heard me say
     in the presence of many witnesses
entrust to reliable men
who will also be qualified to teach others.   2 TIMOTHY 2:1,2

The king read in their hearing
all the words of the book of the covenant,
which had been found in the temple of the Lord.
The king stood by the pillar
and renewed the covenant in the presence of the Lord –
to follow the Lord
and keep his commands, regulations and decrees
with all his heart and all his soul,
thus confirming the words of the covenant
     written in this book.
Then all the people pledged themselves to the covenant.

                  2 KINGS 23:2,3

Examples of leadership

Since then
no prophet has risen in Israel like Moses,
whom the Lord knew face to face,
who did all those miraculous signs and wonders
      the Lord sent him to do in Egypt –
to Pharaoh and to all his officials
      and to his whole land.
For no-one has ever shown the mighty power
      or performed the awesome deeds
that Moses did in the sight of all Israel.

DEUTERONOMY 34:10–12

Josiah got rid of the mediums and spiritists,
the household gods,
the idols and all the other detestable things
      seen in Judah and Jerusalem. . .
Neither before nor after Josiah
was there a king like him
who turned to the Lord as he did –
with all his heart and with all his soul
      and with all his strength,
in accordance with all the Law of Moses.   2 KINGS 23:24,25

They came to Capernaum.
When Jesus was in the house, he asked them,
'What were you arguing about on the road?'
But they kept quiet
because on the way
they had argued about who was the greatest.
Sitting down, Jesus called the Twelve and said,
'If anyone wants to be first,
he must be the very last,
and the servant of all.'

MARK 9:33–35

The people's need

So they were scattered
because there was no shepherd,
and when they were scattered
they became food for all the wild animals.
My sheep wandered over all the mountains
and on every high hill.
They were scattered over the whole earth,
and no-one searched or looked for them.   EZEKIEL 34:5,6

When Jesus landed and saw a large crowd,
he had compassion on them,
because they were like sheep without a shepherd.
So he began teaching them many things.   MARK 6:34

Go . . . to the lost sheep of Israel.
As you go, preach this message:
'The kingdom of heaven is near.'
Heal the sick, raise the dead,
cleanse those who have leprosy,
drive out demons.
Freely you have received, freely give.   MATTHEW 10:6–8

Follow me!

As Jesus walked beside the Sea of Galilee,
he saw Simon and his brother Andrew
casting a net into the lake,
for they were fishermen.
'Come, follow me,' Jesus said,
'and I will make you fishers of men.'
At once they left their nets and followed him.
When he had gone a little farther,
he saw James son of Zebedee and his brother John
    in a boat,
preparing their nets.
Without delay he called them,
and they left their father Zebedee in the boat
    with the hired men
and followed him.   MARK 1:16–20

As he walked along,
he saw Levi son of Alphaeus
sitting at the tax collector's booth.
'Follow me,' Jesus told him,
and Levi got up and followed him.   MARK 2:14

The next day Jesus decided to leave for Galilee.
Finding Philip, he said to him,
'Follow me.'
Philip found Nathanael and told him,
'We have found the one Moses wrote about in the Law,
and about whom the prophets also wrote –
Jesus of Nazareth, the son of Joseph.'
When Jesus saw Nathanael approaching,
he said of him,
'Here is a true Israelite,
in whom there is nothing false.'   JOHN 1:43,45,47

The people God chooses

Amos answered Amaziah,
'I was neither a prophet nor a prophet's son,
but I was a shepherd,
and I also took care of sycamore fig-trees.
But the Lord took me from tending the flock
and said to me,
"Go, prophesy to my people Israel." '

AMOS 7:14,15

Brothers,
think of what you were when you were called.
Not many of you were wise by human standards;
not many were influential;
not many were of noble birth.
But God chose the foolish things of the world
to shame the wise;
God chose the weak things of the world
to shame the strong.
He chose the lowly things of this world
and the despised things –
and the things that are not –
to nullify the things that are,
so that no-one may boast before him.
It is because of him that you are in Christ Jesus,
who has become for us wisdom from God –
that is, our righteousness, holiness and redemption.
Therefore, as it is written:
'Let him who boasts boast in the Lord.'

1 CORINTHIANS 1:26–31

The people God uses

Moses said to the Lord,
'O Lord, I have never been eloquent,
neither in the past
nor since you have spoken to your servant.
I am slow of speech and tongue.'
The Lord said to him,
'Who gave man his mouth?
Who makes him deaf or dumb?
Who gives him sight or makes him blind?
Is it not I, the Lord?
Now go. . .'   EXODUS 4:10,11,12

Restore to me the joy of your salvation
and grant me a willing spirit, to sustain me.
Then I will teach transgressors your ways,
and sinners will turn back to you.
Save me from bloodguiltiness, O God,
the God who saves me,
and my tongue will sing of your righteousness.
O Lord, open my lips,
and my mouth will declare your praise.   PSALM 51:12–15

When I came to you, brothers,
I did not come with eloquence or superior wisdom
as I proclaimed to you the testimony about God.
I came to you in weakness and fear,
and with much trembling.
My message and my preaching
were not with wise and persuasive words,
but with a demonstration of the Spirit's power,
so that your faith might not rest on men's wisdom,
but on God's power.   1 CORINTHIANS 2:1,3–5

The authority given to God's leaders

Moses said to God,
'Suppose I go to the Israelites and say to them,
"The God of your fathers has sent me to you,"
and they ask me,
"What is his name?"
Then what shall I tell them?'
God said to Moses,
'I am who I am.
This is what you are to say to the Israelites:
"I AM has sent me to you." '   EXODUS 3:13,14

Then Jesus came to them and said,
'All authority in heaven and on earth
    has been given to me.
Therefore go and make disciples of all nations,
baptising them in the name of the Father
and of the Son and of the Holy Spirit,
and teaching them
to obey everything I have commanded you.
And surely I will be with you always,
to the very end of the age.'   MATTHEW 28:18–20

I no longer call you servants,
because a servant does not know his master's business.
Instead, I have called you friends,
for everything that I learned from my Father
I have made known to you.
You did not choose me,
but I chose you to go and bear fruit –
fruit that will last.
Then the Father will give you
    whatever you ask in my name.   JOHN 15:15,16

God's early preparation

The word of the Lord came to me, saying,
'Before I formed you in the womb I knew you,
before you were born I set you apart;
I appointed you as a prophet to the nations.
Do not say, "I am only a child."
You must go to everyone I send you to
and say whatever I command you.
Do not be afraid of them,
for I am with you and will rescue you,'
declares the Lord.   JEREMIAH 1:4,5,7,8

But David said to Saul,
'Your servant has been keeping his father's sheep.
When a lion or a bear came
and carried off a sheep from the flock,
I went after it,
struck it and rescued the sheep from its mouth.
The Lord who delivered me
from the paw of the lion and the paw of the bear
will deliver me from the hand of this Philistine.'
                    1 SAMUEL 17:34,35,37

The Lord was with Samuel as he grew up,
and he let none of his words fall to the ground.
And all Israel from Dan to Beersheba
recognised that Samuel was attested
        as a prophet of the Lord.
The Lord continued to appear at Shiloh,
and there he revealed himself to Samuel
        through his word.   1 SAMUEL 3:19–21

The need for perseverance

Jesus said to another man, 'Follow me.'
But the man replied, 'Lord,
first let me go and bury my father.'
Jesus said to him,
'Let the dead bury their own dead,
but you go and proclaim the kingdom of God.'
Still another said, 'I will follow you, Lord;
but first let me go back
    and say good-bye to my family.'
Jesus replied,
'No-one who puts his hand to the plough
    and looks back
is fit for service in the kingdom of God.'   LUKE 9:59–62

I have fought the good fight,
I have finished the race, I have kept the faith.
Now there is in store for me
the crown of righteousness,
which the Lord, the righteous Judge,
will award to me on that day –
and not only to me,
but also to all who have longed for his appearing.
Do your best to come to me quickly,
for Demas, because he loved this world,
has deserted me and has gone to Thessalonica.
At my first defence, no-one came to my support,
but everyone deserted me.
May it not be held against them.
But the Lord stood at my side and gave me strength. . .
The Lord will rescue me from every evil attack
and will bring me safely to his heavenly kingdom.
To him be the glory for ever and ever. Amen.
                    2 TIMOTHY 4:7–10,16,17,18

Preaching despite unpopularity

The word of the Lord came to Elijah the Tishbite:
'Go down to meet Ahab king of Israel,
who rules in Samaria.
He is now in Naboth's vineyard,
where he has gone to take possession of it.'
Ahab said to Elijah,
'So you have found me, my enemy!'
'I have found you,' he answered,
'because you have sold yourself
to do evil in the eyes of the Lord.'   1 KINGS 21:17,18,20

In the presence of God and of Christ Jesus,
who will judge the living and the dead,
and in view of his appearing and his kingdom,
I give you this charge:
Preach the Word;
be prepared in season and out of season;
correct, rebuke and encourage –
with great patience and careful instruction.
Keep your head in all situations,
endure hardship,
do the work of an evangelist,
discharge all the duties of your ministry.   2 TIMOTHY 4:1,2,5

I will speak of your statues before kings
and will not be put to shame,
for I delight in your commandments
because I love them.   PSALM 119:46,47

Then the word of the Lord came to Elijah the Tishbite:
'Have you noticed
how Ahab has humbled himself before me?'   1 KINGS 21:28,29

God's way may not be ours

O Lord, you deceived me, and I was deceived,
you overpowered me and prevailed.
I am ridiculed all day long; everyone mocks me.
But if I say, 'I will not mention him
or speak any more in his name,'
his word is in my heart like a burning fire,
shut up in my bones.
I am weary of holding it in;
indeed, I cannot.   JEREMIAH 20:7,9

But Jonah was greatly displeased and became angry.
He prayed to the Lord,
'O Lord, is this not what I said
when I was still at home?
That is why I was so quick to flee to Tarshish.
I knew that you are a gracious and compassionate God,
slow to anger and abounding in love,
a God who relents from sending calamity.
Now, O Lord, take away my life,
for it is better for me to die than to live.'   JONAH 4:1–3

I know that you can do all things;
no plan of yours can be thwarted.
You asked, 'Who is this that obscures my counsel
    without knowledge?'
Surely I spoke of things I did not understand,
things too wonderful for me to know.
You said, 'Listen now, and I will speak;
I will question you, and you shall answer me.'
My ears had heard of you but now my eyes have seen you.
Therefore I despise myself
and repent in dust and ashes.   JOB 42:2–6

Danger and difficulty

As they were walking along the road,
a man said to Jesus,
'I will follow you wherever you go.'
Jesus replied,
'Foxes have holes and birds of the air have nests,
but the Son of Man has no place to lay his head.'

LUKE 9:57,58

I have been constantly on the move.
I have been in danger from rivers,
in danger from bandits,
in danger from my own countrymen,
in danger from Gentiles;
in danger in the city,
in danger in the country,
in danger at sea;
and in danger from false brothers.
I have laboured and toiled
and have often gone without sleep;
I have known hunger and thirst
and have often gone without food;
I have been cold and naked.
Besides everything else,
I face daily the pressure of my concern
      for all the churches.
Who is weak, and I do not feel weak?
Who is led into sin,
and I do not inwardly burn?   2 CORINTHIANS 11:26–29

The Lord is a refuge for the oppressed,
a stronghold in times of trouble.
Those who know your name will trust in you,
for you, Lord, have never forsaken those who seek you.

PSALM 9:9,10

Hardship

As John's disciples were leaving,
Jesus began to speak to the crowd about John:
'What did you go out into the desert to see?
A reed swayed by the wind?
If not, what did you go out to see?
A man dressed in fine clothes?
No, those who wear fine clothes are in kings' palaces.
Then what did you go out to see?
A prophet?
Yes, I tell you, and more than a prophet.'   MATTHEW 11:7–9

Who shall separate us from the love of Christ?
Shall trouble or hardship
or persecution or famine
or nakedness or danger or sword?
As it is written:
'For your sake we face death all day long;
we are considered as sheep to be slaughtered.'
No, in all these things we are more than conquerors
      through him who loved us.   ROMANS 8:35–37

For the Lord God is a sun and shield;
the Lord bestows favour and honour;
no good thing does he withhold
      from those whose walk is blameless.
O Lord Almighty,
blessed is the man who trusts in you.   PSALM 84:11,12

In hardship – dependent on God

Then the word of the Lord came to Elijah:
'Leave here, turn eastwards
and hide in the ravine of Kerith, east of the Jordan.'
So he did what the Lord had told him.
He went to the ravine of Kerith, east of the Jordan,
and stayed there.
The ravens brought him bread and meat in the morning
and bread and meat in the evening,
and he drank from the brook.   1 KINGS 17:2,3,5,6

I have learned to be content
whatever the circumstances.
I know what it is to be in need,
and I know what it is to have plenty.
I have learned the secret of being content
in any and every situation,
whether well fed or hungry,
whether living in plenty or in want.
I can do everything through him
        who gives me strength.   PHILIPPIANS 4:11,12,13

Calling the Twelve to him,
Jesus sent them out two by two
and gave them authority over evil spirits.
These were his instructions:
'Take nothing for the journey except a staff –
no bread, no bag, no money in your belts.
Wear sandals but not an extra tunic.'
They went out and preached that people should repent.

MARK 6:7–9,12

Reflecting the light

When they saw the courage of Peter and John
and realised that they were unschooled, ordinary men,
they were astonished and they took note
    that these men had been with Jesus.   ACTS 4:13

For we do not preach ourselves,
but Jesus Christ as Lord,
and ourselves as your servants for Jesus' sake.
For God, who said,
'Let light shine out of darkness,'
made his light shine in our hearts
to give us
the light of the knowledge of the glory of God
in the face of Christ.
But we have this treasure in jars of clay
to show that this all-surpassing power is from God
and not from us.   2 CORINTHIANS 4:5–7

In him was life,
and that life was the light of men.
The light shines in the darkness,
but the darkness has not understood it.
The Word became flesh
and lived for a while among us.
We have seen his glory,
the glory of the one and only Son,
who came from the Father,
full of grace and truth.   JOHN 1:4,5,14

Standing firm for the truth

You must be on your guard.
You will be handed over to the local councils
and flogged in the synagogues.
On account of me
you will stand before governors and kings
as witnesses to them.
Whenever you are arrested and brought to trial,
do not worry beforehand about what to say.
Just say whatever is given you at the time,
for it is not you speaking, but the Holy Spirit.   MARK 13:9,11

This is what the Lord says:
Do what is just and right.
Rescue from the hand of his oppressor
the one who has been robbed.
Do no wrong or violence to the alien,
the fatherless or the widow,
and do not shed innocent blood in this place.
But if you do not obey these commands,
      declares the Lord,
I swear by myself
that this palace will become a ruin.   JEREMIAH 22:3,5

Always be prepared to give an answer
to everyone who asks you to give the reason
      for the hope that you have.
But do this with gentleness and respect,
keeping a clear conscience,
so that those who speak maliciously
against your good behaviour in Christ
may be ashamed of their slander.   1 PETER 3:15,16

Public witness to faith

I hear many whispering,
'Terror on every side!
Report him! Let's report him!'
All my friends are waiting for me to slip, saying,
'Perhaps he will be deceived;
then we will prevail over him
and take our revenge on him.'   JEREMIAH 20:10

A time is coming
when anyone who kills you
will think he is offering a service to God.
They will do such things
because they have not known the Father or me.
I have told you this,
so that when the time comes
you will remember that I warned you. . .   JOHN 16:2,3,4

As servants of God
we commend ourselves in every way:
in great endurance;
in troubles, hardships and distresses;
in beatings, imprisonments and riots;
in hard work, sleepless nights and hunger.
Through glory and dishonour,
bad report and good report;
genuine, yet regarded as impostors;
known, yet regarded as unknown;
dying, and yet we live on;
beaten, and yet not killed.   2 CORINTHIANS 6:4,5,8,9

God's word and his kingdom

Those who accepted his message
    were baptised,
and about three thousand
were added to their number that day.
Everyone was filled with awe,
and many wonders and miraculous signs
were done by the apostles.
And the Lord added to their number daily
those who were being saved.   ACTS 2:41,43,47

All over the world
this gospel is producing fruit and growing,
just as it has been doing among you
since the day you heard it
and understood God's grace in all its truth.
For he has rescued us from the dominion of darkness
and brought us into the kingdom
    of the Son he loves.
        COLOSSIANS 1:6,13

Again he said,
'What shall we say the kingdom of God is like,
or what parable shall we use to describe it?
It is like a mustard seed,
which is the smallest seed
    you plant in the ground.
Yet when planted, it grows
and becomes the largest of all garden plants,
with such big branches
that the birds of the air
    can perch in its shade.'
        MARK 4:30–32

Hear the good news!

The beginning of the gospel
about Jesus Christ, the Son of God.
It is written in Isaiah the prophet:
'I will send my messenger ahead of you,
who will prepare your way –
a voice of one calling in the desert,
"Prepare the way for the Lord,
make straight paths for him." '   MARK 1:1–3

Now, brothers, I want to remind you
      of the gospel I preached to you,
which you received
and on which you have taken your stand.
By this gospel you are saved,
if you hold firmly
      to the word I preached to you.
Otherwise, you have believed in vain.
For what I received I passed on to you
      as of first importance:
that Christ died for our sins
according to the Scriptures,
that he was buried,
that he was raised on the third day
according to the Scriptures.
This is what we preach,
and this is what you believed.   1 CORINTHIANS 15:1–4,11

When I came to you, brothers,
I did not come with eloquence or superior wisdom
      as I proclaimed to you the testimony about God.
For I resolved to know nothing while I was with you
except Jesus Christ and him crucified.   1 CORINTHIANS 2:1,2

Hear – and obey!

Do not merely listen to the word,
and so deceive yourselves.
Do what it says.
The man who looks intently
    into the perfect law that gives freedom,
and continues to do this,
not forgetting what he has heard,
    but doing it –
he will be blessed in what he does.   JAMES 1:22,25

Not everyone who says to me, 'Lord, Lord,'
will enter the kingdom of heaven,
but only he who does the will of my Father
    who is in heaven.
Many will say to me on that day,
'Lord, Lord, did we not prophesy in your name,
and in your name drive out demons
and perform many miracles?'
Then I will tell them plainly,
'I never knew you.
Away from me, you evildoers!'   MATTHEW 7:21–23

Despising God's word

Coming to his home town,
he began teaching the people in their synagogue,
and they were amazed.
'Where did this man get this wisdom
and these miraculous powers?' they asked.
'Isn't this the carpenter's son?
Isn't his mother's name Mary,
and aren't his brothers James, Joseph,
     Simon and Judas?
Aren't all his sisters with us?
Where then did this man get all these things?'
And they took offence at him.
But Jesus said to them,
'Only in his home town and in his own house
is a prophet without honour.'
And he did not do many miracles there
because of their lack of faith.   MATTHEW 13:54–58

The temple guards
went back to the chief priests and Pharisees,
who asked them,
'Why didn't you bring him in?'
'No-one ever spoke the way this man does,'
the guards declared.
'You mean he has deceived you also?'
the Pharisee retorted.
'Has any of the rulers
or of the Pharisees believed in him?
No! But this mob that knows nothing of the law –
there is a curse on them.'   JOHN 7:45–49

Pictures of the word in action

The seed is the word of God.
The seed on good soil
stands for those with a noble and good heart,
who hear the word, retain it,
and by persevering produce a crop.   LUKE 8:11,15

As the rain and the snow come down from heaven,
and do not return to it without watering the earth
and making it bud and flourish,
so that it yields seed for the sower
     and bread for the eater,
so is my word that goes out from my mouth:
It will not return to me empty,
but will accomplish what I desire
and achieve the purpose for which I sent it.   ISAIAH 55:10,11

The word of God is living and active.
Sharper than any double-edged sword,
it penetrates even to dividing soul and spirit,
     joints and marrow;
it judges the thoughts and attitudes of the heart.
Nothing in all creation is hidden from God's sight.
Everything is uncovered and laid bare
before the eyes of him
     to whom we must give account.

     HEBREWS 4:12,13

'Is not my word like fire,' declares the Lord,
'and like a hammer that breaks a rock in pieces?'

     JEREMIAH 23:29

The word cannot be silenced

Does a lion roar in the thicket
when he has no prey?
Does he growl in his den
when he has caught nothing?
The lion has roared –
who will not fear?
The Sovereign Lord has spoken –
who can but prophesy?   AMOS 3:4,8

They ordered them to withdraw
    from the Sanhedrin
and then conferred together.
'. . .We must warn these men
to speak no longer to anyone in this name.'
Then they called them in again
and commanded them not to speak or teach at all
    in the name of Jesus.
But Peter and John replied,
'Judge for yourselves
    whether it is right in God's sight
to obey you rather than God.
For we cannot help speaking
about what we have seen and heard.'
After further threats
they let them go.
They could not decide how to punish them,
because all the people were praising God
for what had happened.   ACTS 4:15,17–21

God's word through the Scriptures

The king called together
all the elders of Judah and Jerusalem.
He went up to the temple of the Lord
with the men of Judah,
the people of Jerusalem,
the priests and the prophets –
all the people from the least to the greatest.
He read in their hearing
all the words of the book of the covenant,
which had been found in the temple
    of the Lord.
Then all the people pledged themselves
    to the covenant.   2 KINGS 23:1,2,3

The law of the Lord is perfect,
reviving the soul.
The statutes of the Lord are trustworthy,
making wise the simple.
The precepts of the Lord are right,
giving joy to the heart.
The commands of the Lord are radiant,
giving light to the eyes.
The fear of the Lord is pure,
enduring for ever.
The ordinances of the Lord are sure
and altogether righteous.
They are more precious than gold,
    than much pure gold;
they are sweeter than honey,
    than honey from the comb.
By them is your servant warned;
in keeping them there is great reward.   PSALM 19:7–11

Proclaiming the word of God

Then the eleven disciples went to Galilee,
to the mountain where Jesus had told them to go.
When they saw him, they worshipped him;
but some doubted.
Then Jesus came to them and said,
'All authority in heaven and on earth
    has been given to me.
Therefore go and make disciples
    of all nations,
baptising them in the name of the Father
    and of the Son and of the Holy Spirit,
and teaching them to obey
everything I have commanded you.'   MATTHEW 28:16–20

Make known among the nations what he has done,
and proclaim that his name is exalted.
Sing to the Lord,
for he has done glorious things;
let this be known to all the world.   ISAIAH 12:4,5

Worship the Lord
in the splendour of his holiness;
tremble before him, all the earth.
Say among the nations,
'The Lord reigns.'
Then all the trees of the forest will sing for joy;
they will sing before the Lord, for he comes,
he comes to judge the earth.
He will judge the world in righteousness
and the peoples in his truth.   PSALM 96:9,10,12,13

Our duty to proclaim his word

You are the salt of the earth.
But if the salt loses its saltiness,
how can it be made salty again?
It is no longer good for anything,
except to be thrown out and trampled by men.
You are the light of the world.
A city on a hill cannot be hidden.
Neither do people light a lamp
　　and put it under a bowl.
Instead they put it on its stand,
and it gives light to everyone in the house.
In the same way,
let your light shine before men. MATTHEW 5:13–16

How, then, can they call on the one
　　they have not believed in?
And how can they believe in the one
　　of whom they have not heard?
And how can they hear
without someone preaching to them?
And how can they preach
unless they are sent?
As it is written,
'How beautiful are the feet of those
　　who bring good news!'
But not all the Israelites accepted the good news.
For Isaiah says,
'Lord, who has believed our message?'
Consequently,
faith comes from hearing the message,
and the message is heard
through the word of Christ. ROMANS 10:14–17

God's love for his own people

It was I who taught Ephraim to walk,
taking them by the arms;
but they did not realise it was I who healed them.
I led them with cords of human kindness,
with ties of love;
I lifted the yoke from their neck
and bent down to feed them.
How can I give up, Ephraim?
How can I hand you over, Israel?   HOSEA 11:3,4,8

Zion said,
'The Lord has forsaken me,
the Lord has forgotten me.'
This is what the Lord says:
'Can a mother forget the baby at her breast
and have no compassion on the child she has borne?
Though she may forget, I will not forget you!
See, I have engraved you on the palms of my hands;
your walls are ever before me.'   ISAIAH 49:14–16

O Jerusalem, Jerusalem,
you who kill the prophets
and stone those sent to you,
how often I have longed
to gather your children together,
as a hen gathers her chicks under her wings,
but you were not willing.
I tell you, you will not see me again
until you say,
'Blessed is he who comes
    in the name of the Lord.'   MATTHEW 23:37,39

True religion

Lord, who may dwell in your sanctuary?
Who may live on your holy hill?
He whose walk is blameless
and who does what is righteous,
who speaks the truth from his heart
and has no slander on his tongue,
who does his neighbour no wrong
and casts no slur on his fellow man,
who despises a vile man
but honours those who fear the Lord,
who keeps his oath
even when it hurts.   PSALM 15:1–4

If you really change your ways and your actions
and deal with each other justly,
if you do not oppress the alien,
the fatherless or the widow
and do not shed innocent blood in this place . . .
then I will let you live in this place,
in the land I gave to your forefathers
for ever and ever.   JEREMIAH 7:5,6,7

Religion that God our Father
      accepts as pure and faultless
in this:
to look after orphans and widows
      in their distress
and to keep oneself from being polluted
      by the world.   JAMES 1:27

December 3rd   The nations before God

Easy answers and false peace

'From the least to the greatest,
all are greedy for gain;
prophets and priests alike, all practise deceit.
They dress the wound of my people
as though it were not serious.
"Peace, peace," they say,
when there is no peace.
Are they ashamed of their loathsome conduct?
No, they have no shame at all;
they do not even know how to blush.
So they will fall among the fallen . . . '
says the Lord.   JEREMIAH 6:13–15

This is what the Lord says:
'As for the prophets who lead my people astray,
if one feeds them, they proclaim "peace";
if he does not, they prepare
        to wage war against him.'
But as for me, I am filled with power,
with the Spirit of the Lord,
and with justice and might,
to declare to Jacob his transgression,
to Israel his sin.   MICAH 3:5,8

The time will come
when men will not put up with sound doctrine.
Instead, to suit their own desires,
they will gather around them
a great number of teachers
to say what their itching ears want to hear.
They will turn their ears away from the truth
and turn aside to myths.   2 TIMOTHY 4:3,4

The choice before a people

Then they believed his promises
and sang his praise.
But they soon forgot what he had done
and did not wait for his counsel.
In the desert they gave in to their craving;
in the waste-land they put God to the test.
So he gave them what they asked for,
but sent a wasting disease upon them.   PSALM 106:12–15

Gather together, gather together,
O shameful nation,
before the appointed time arrives
and that day sweeps on like chaff,
before the fierce anger of the Lord comes upon you,
before the day of the Lord's wrath comes upon you.
Seek the Lord,
all you humble of the land,
you who do what he commands.
Seek righteousness, seek humility;
perhaps you will be sheltered
on the day of the Lord's anger.   ZEPHANIAH 2:1–3

This day I call heaven and earth
as witnesses against you
that I have set before you life and death,
blessings and curses.
Now choose life,
so that you and your children may live
and that you may love the Lord your God,
listen to his voice, and hold fast to him.
For the Lord is your life,
and he will give you many years in the land
      he swore to give to your fathers.
          DEUTERONOMY 30:19,20

An ungodly city

Jesus said to his disciples:
'Things that cause people to sin are bound to come,
but woe to that person through whom they come.
It would be better for him to be thrown into the sea
with a millstone tied round his neck
than for him to cause one of these little ones to sin.
So watch yourselves. . .'   LUKE 17:1–3

I saw another angel coming down from heaven.
He had great authority,
and the earth was illuminated by his splendour.
With a mighty voice he shouted:
'Fallen! Fallen is Babylon the Great!'
Then I heard another voice from heaven say:
'Come out of her, my people,
so that you will not share in her sins,
so that you will not receive any of her plagues;
for her sins are piled up to heaven,
and God has remembered her crimes.'
Then a mighty angel picked up a boulder
        the size of a large millstone
and threw it into the sea, and said:
'With such violence
the great city of Babylon will be thrown down,
never to be found again.'   REVELATION 18:1,2,4,5,21

Impending judgement

'You have said harsh things against me,'
says the Lord.
'Yet you ask, "What have we said against you?"
You have said, "It is futile to serve God.
What did we gain by carrying out his requirements
and going about like mourners
        before the Lord Almighty?
But now we call the arrogant blessed.
Certainly the evildoers prosper,
and even those who challenge God escape." '
Then those who feared the Lord talked with each other,
and the Lord listened and heard.
A scroll of remembrance was written in his presence
concerning those who feared the Lord
        and honoured his name.
'They will be mine,' says the Lord Almighty,
'in the day when I make up my treasured possession.'
I will spare them,
just as in compassion a man spares his son
        who serves him.'   MALACHI 3:13–17

Then I saw a great white throne
and him who was seated on it.
Earth and sky fled from his presence,
and there was no place for them.
And I saw the dead, great and small,
standing before the throne,
and books were opened.
Another book was opened, which is the book of life.
The dead were judged
        according to what they had done
as recorded in the books.   REVELATION 20:11,12

December 7th   The nations before God

The promise of peace

I will listen to what God the Lord will say;
he promises peace to his people, his saints –
but let them not return to folly.
Surely his salvation is near those who fear him,
that his glory may dwell in our land.   PSALM 85:8,9

And I heard a loud voice from the throne saying,
'Now the dwelling of God is with men,
and he will live with them.
They will be his people,
and God himself will be with them
and be their God.
He will wipe every tear from their eyes.
There will be no more death or mourning
     or crying or pain,
for the old order of things has passed away.'
     REVELATION 21:3,4

Love and faithfulness meet together;
righteousness and peace kiss each other.
Faithfulness springs forth from the earth,
and righteousness looks down from heaven.   PSALM 85:10,11

The coming of the Son of Man

The Lord reigns, let the earth be glad;
let the distant shores rejoice.
Clouds and thick darkness surround him;
righteousness and justice
    are the foundation of his throne.
Fire goes before him
and consumes his foe on every side.
His lightning lights up the world;
the earth sees and trembles.
The mountains melt like wax before the Lord,
before the Lord of all the earth.
The heavens proclaim his righteousness,
and all the peoples see his glory.   PSALM 97:1–6

For as the lightning comes from the east
    and flashes to the west,
so will be the coming of the Son of Man.
Immediately after the distress of those days
'the sun will be darkened,
and the moon will not give its light;
the stars will fall from the sky,
and the heavenly bodies will be shaken.'
At that time
the sign of the Son of Man will appear in the sky,
and all the nations of the earth will mourn.
They will see the Son of Man coming
    on the clouds of the sky,
with power and great glory.   MATTHEW 24:27,29,30

The day of the Lord

Go into the rocks, hide in the ground
from dread of the Lord
and the splendour of his majesty!
The eyes of the arrogant man will be humbled
and the pride of men brought low;
the Lord alone will be exalted in that day.
The Lord Almighty
    has a day in store for all the proud and lofty,
for all that is exalted
(and they will be humbled).
The arrogance of man will be brought low
and the pride of men humbled;
the Lord alone will be exalted in that day.   ISAIAH 2:10–12,17

The stars in the sky fell to earth,
as late figs drop from a fig-tree
    when shaken by a strong wind.
The sky receded like a scroll, rolling up,
and every mountain and island
was removed from its place.
Then the kings of the earth,
the princes, the generals, the rich, the mighty,
and every slave and every free man
hid in caves and among the rocks of the mountains.
                    REVELATION 6:13–15

Jesus told them this parable:
'Look at the fig-tree and all the trees.
When they sprout leaves,
you can see for yourselves and know
    that summer is near.
Even so,
when you see these things happening,
you know that the kingdom of God is near.'   LUKE 21:29–31

Waiting in hope

That is how it will be
    at the coming of the Son of Man.
Two men will be in the field;
one will be taken and the other left.
Two women will be grinding with a hand mill;
one will be taken and the other left.
Therefore keep watch,
because you do not know on what day
    your Lord will come.   MATTHEW 24:39–42

In that day men will throw away
    to the rodents and bats
their idols of silver and idols of gold,
which they made to worship.
They will flee to caverns in the rocks
and to the overhanging crags
from dread of the Lord
and the splendour of his majesty,
when he rises to shake the earth.
Stop trusting in man,
who has but a breath in his nostrils.
Of what account is he?   ISAIAH 2:20–22

For the grace of God that brings salvation
    has appeared to all men.
It teaches us to say 'No' to ungodliness
and worldly passions,
and to live self-controlled, upright and godly lives
    in this present age,
while we wait for the blessed hope –
the glorious appearing of our great God and Saviour,
Jesus Christ.   TITUS 2:11–13

Our responsibility to God

Once the owner of the house gets up
    and closes the door,
you will stand outside knocking and pleading,
'Sir, open the door for us,'
But he will answer,
'I don't know you or where you come from.'
Then you will say,
'We ate and drank with you,
    and you taught in our streets.'
But he will reply,
'I don't know you or where you come from.
Away from me, all you evildoers!'   LUKE 13:25–27

Let us consider
    how we may spur one another on
towards love and good deeds.
Let us not give up meeting together,
as some are in the habit of doing,
but let us encourage one another –
and all the more as you see the Day approaching.
If we deliberately keep on sinning
    after we have received the knowledge of the truth,
no sacrifice for sins is left,
but only a fearful expectation of judgement
and of raging fire
that will consume the enemies of God.   HEBREWS 10:24–27

The vision of the coming Christ

Ascribe to the Lord, O families of nations,
ascribe to the Lord glory and strength.
Ascribe to the Lord the glory due to his name;
bring an offering and come into his courts.
Worship the Lord in the splendour of his holiness;
tremble before him, all the earth.
Let the heavens rejoice, let the earth be glad;
let the sea resound, and all that is in it;
let the fields be jubilant, and everything in them.
Then all the trees of the forest will sing for joy;
they will sing before the Lord, for he comes,
he comes to judge the earth.
He will judge the world in righteousness
and the peoples in his truth.   PSALM 96:7–9,11–13

I charge you to keep this commandment
without spot or blame
until the appearing of our Lord Jesus Christ,
which God will bring about in his own time –
God, the blessed and only Ruler,
the King of kings and Lord of lords,
who alone is immortal
and who lives in unapproachable light,
whom no-one has seen or can see.
To him be honour and might for ever. Amen.
                              1 TIMOTHY 6:14–16

At any time

Therefore keep watch,
because you do not know on what day
    your Lord will come.
But understand this:
If the owner of the house had known
at what time of night the thief was coming,
he would have kept watch
and would not have let his house be broken into.
So you also must be ready,
because the Son of Man will come at an hour
    when you do not expect him.   MATTHEW 24:42–44

Now, brothers,
about times and dates
we do not need to write to you,
for you know very well
that the day of the Lord will come
    like a thief in the night.
While people are saying, 'Peace and safety.'
destruction will come on them suddenly,
as labour pains on a pregnant woman,
and they will not escape.
But you, brothers, are not in darkness
so that this day should surprise you like a thief.
You are all sons of the light and sons of the day.
We do not belong to the night or to the darkness.
So then, let us not be like others, who are asleep,
but let us be alert and self-controlled.   1 THESSALONIANS 5:1–6

The sound of his coming

The voice of the Lord is over the waters;
The God of glory thunders,
the Lord thunders over the mighty waters.
The voice of the Lord is powerful;
the voice of the Lord is majestic.   PSALM 29:3,4

At that time the sign of the Son of Man
        will appear in the sky,
and all the nations of the earth will mourn.
They will see the Son of Man coming
        on the clouds of the sky,
with power and great glory.
And he will send his angels with a loud trumpet call,
and they will gather his elect from the four winds,
from one end of the heavens to the other.   MATTHEW 24:30,31

For the Lord himself will come down from heaven,
        with a loud command,
with the voice of the archangel
and with the trumpet call of God,
and the dead in Christ will rise first.   1 THESSALONIANS 4:16

For the trumpet will sound,
the dead will be raised imperishable,
and we will be changed.
For the perishable must clothe itself
        with the imperishable,
and the mortal with immortality.   1 CORINTHIANS 15:52,53

Signs of the times

There will be signs in the sun, moon and stars.
On the earth,
nations will be in anguish and perplexity
    at the roaring and tossing of the sea.
Men will faint from terror,
apprehensive of what is coming on the world,
for the heavenly bodies will be shaken.
At that time they will see the Son of Man
coming in a cloud with power and great glory.
When these things begin to take place,
stand up and lift up your heads,
because your redemption is drawing near.   LUKE 21:25–28

I will show wonders in the heavens
    and on the earth,
blood and fire and billows of smoke.
The sun will be turned to darkness
and the moon to blood
before the coming of the great and dreadful day
    of the Lord.
And everyone who calls on the name of the Lord
will be saved. . .   JOEL 2:30–32

The hour has come
for you to wake up from your slumber,
because our salvation is nearer now
than when we first believed.
The night is nearly over;
the day is almost here.
So let us put aside the deeds of darkness
and put on the armour of light.   ROMANS 13:11,12

Being ready for judgement

Woe to you who long for the day of the Lord!
Why do you long for the day of the Lord?
That day will be darkness, not light.
It will be as though a man fled from a lion
        only to meet a bear,
as though he entered his house
and rested his hand on the wall
only to have a snake bite him.
Will not the day of the Lord be darkness, not light –
pitch-dark, without a ray of brightness?   AMOS 5:18–20

The Word of the Lord came to me:
'Son of Man, take up a lament
concerning Pharaoh King of Egypt
and say to him. . .
"When I snuff you out, I will cover the heavens
and darken their stars;
I will cover the sun with a cloud,
and the moon will not give its light.
All the shining lights in the heavens
        I will darken over you;
I will bring darkness over your land,
declares the Sovereign Lord.
I will trouble the hearts of many peoples
when I bring about your destruction among the nations,
among lands you have not known.
I will cause many peoples to be appalled at you,
and their kings will shudder with horror
        because of you
        when I brandish my sword before them.
On the day of your downfall
each of them will tremble
        every moment for his life." '   EZEKIEL 32:2,7–10

The judgement upon a people

O Jerusalem, Jerusalem,
you who kill the prophets and stone those sent to you,
how often I have longed
    to gather your children together,
as a hen gathers her chicks under her wings,
but you were not willing!
Look, your house is left to you desolate.
I tell you, you will not see me again until you say,
'Blessed is he who comes in the name of the Lord.'

LUKE 13:34,35

Then the Lord said to me . . . 'Speak this word to them:
"Let my eyes overflow with tears
night and day without ceasing;
for my virgin daughter – my people –
has suffered a grievous wound, a crushing blow." '
O Lord, we acknowledge our wickedness
and the guilt of our fathers;
we have indeed sinned against you.
For the sake of your name do not despise us;
do not dishonour your glorious throne.
Remember your covenant with us and do not break it.

JEREMIAH 14:14,17,20,21

As Jesus approached Jerusalem and saw the city,
he wept over it and said,
'If you, even you, had only known on this day
    what would bring you peace –
but now it is hidden from your eyes.
The days will come upon you
when your enemies will build an embankment
    against you
and encircle you and hem you in on every side.
They will not leave one stone on another,
because you did not recognise
the time of God's coming to you.'

LUKE 19:41–43,44

He has set a day

In the past God overlooked such ignorance,
but now he commands all people everywhere to repent.
For he has set a day
    when he will judge the world with justice
by the man he has appointed.
He has given proof of this to all men
by raising him from the dead.   ACTS 17:30,31

Do you think you will escape God's judgement?
Or do you show contempt for the riches of his kindness,
    tolerance and patience,
not realising that God's kindness leads you
    towards repentance?
But because of your stubbornness
and your unrepentant heart,
you are storing up wrath against yourself
for the day of God's wrath,
when his righteous judgement will be revealed.
God 'will give to each person
according to what he has done.'
To those who by persistence in doing good seek glory,
    honour and immortality,
he will give eternal life.
But for those who are self-seeking
and who reject the truth and follow evil,
there will be wrath and anger.   ROMANS 2:3–8

Coming into the light

This is the verdict:
Light has come into the world,
but men loved darkness instead of light
because their deeds were evil.
Everyone who does evil hates the light,
and will not come into the light
for fear that his deeds will be exposed.
But whoever lives by the truth comes into the light,
so that it may be seen plainly
that what he has done has been done through God.

JOHN 3:19–21

Therefore judge nothing before the appointed time;
wait till the Lord comes.
He will bring to light what is hidden in darkness
and will expose the motives of men's hearts.
At that time each will receive his praise from God.

1 CORINTHIANS 4:5

God is light;
in him there is no darkness at all.
If we claim to have fellowship with him
yet walk in the darkness,
we lie and do not live by the truth.   1 JOHN 1:5,6

The night is nearly over;
the day is almost here.
So let us put aside the deeds of darkness
and put on the armour of light.
Let us behave decently, as in the daytime,
not in orgies and drunkenness,
not in sexual immorality and debauchery,
not in dissension and jealousy.
Rather, clothe yourselves with the Lord Jesus Christ,
and do not think about how to gratify
    the desires of the sinful nature.   ROMANS 13:12–14

Escaping judgement

For it is time for judgement to begin
    with the family of God;
and if it begins with us,
what will the outcome be
for those who do not obey the gospel of God?   1 PETER 4:17

Nothing in all creation
is hidden from God's sight.
Everything is uncovered and laid bare
before the eyes of him
to whom we must give account.   HEBREWS 4:13

Aaron did as Moses said,
and ran into the midst of the assembly.
The plague had already started among the people,
but Aaron offered the incense
and made atonement for them.
He stood between the living and the dead,
and the plague stopped.   NUMBERS 16:47,48

See to it that you do not refuse him who speaks.
If they did not escape
when they refused him who warned them on earth,
how much less will we,
if we turn away from him
    who warns us from heaven?
Therefore, since we are receiving a kingdom
    that cannot be shaken,
let us be thankful,
and so worship God acceptably with reverence and awe,
for our God is a consuming fire.   HEBREWS 12:25,28,29

Being ready for liberty

God also said to Moses. . .
'Say to the Israelites:
"I am the Lord
and I will bring you out
    from under the yoke of the Egyptians.
I will free you from being slaves to them
and will redeem you with an outstretched arm
and with mighty acts of judgement.
I will take you as my own people,
and I will be your God.
Then you will know that I am the Lord your God,
who brought you out
    from under the yoke of the Egyptians." '   EXODUS 6:2,6,7

The creation waits in eager expectation
    for the sons of God to be revealed.
For the creation was subjected to frustration,
not by its own choice,
but by the will of the one who subjected it,
in hope that the creation itself
    will be liberated from its bondage to decay
and brought into the glorious freedom
of the children of God.
We know that the whole creation has been groaning
    as in the pains of childbirth
right up to the present time.
Not only so, but we ourselves
who have the firstfruits of the Spirit,
grown inwardly
as we wait eagerly for our adoption as sons,
the redemption of our bodies.   ROMANS 8:19–23

The glorious light

Comfort, comfort my people, says your God.
Speak tenderly to Jerusalem, and proclaim to her. . .
that her sin has been paid for. . .
A voice of one calling:
'In the desert prepare the way for the Lord:
make straight in the wilderness
a highway for our God.
Every valley shall be raised up,
every mountain and hill made low;
the rough ground shall become level,
the rugged places a plain.
And the glory of the Lord will be revealed,
and all mankind together will see it.'   ISAIAH 40:1,2,3–5

John's father Zechariah
was filled with the Holy Spirit
and prophesied:
'Praise be to the Lord, the God of Israel,
because he has come
and has redeemed his people.
He has raised up a horn of salvation for us
in the house of his servant David.
And you, my child . . . will go on before the Lord
to prepare the way for him,
to give his people the knowledge of salvation
through the forgiveness of their sins,
because of the tender mercy of our God,
by which the rising sun will come to us from heaven
to shine on those living in darkness
and in the shadow of death,
to guide our feet into the path of peace.'
                                        LUKE 1:67–69, 76–79

Prepare the way!

This is he who was spoken of
through the prophet Isaiah:
'A voice of one calling in the desert,
"Prepare the way for the Lord,
make straight paths for him." '
People went out to him from Jerusalem and all Judea
and the whole region of the Jordan.
Confessing their sins,
they were baptised by him in the Jordan River.

MATTHEW 3:3,5,6

'Build up, build up, prepare the road!
Remove the obstacles out of the way of my people.'
For this is what the high and lofty One says –
he who lives for ever, whose name is holy:
'I live in a high and holy place,
but also with him who is contrite
and lowly in spirit.'

ISAIAH 57:14,15

I will listen to what God the Lord will say;
he promises peace to his people, his saints –
but let them not return to folly.
Surely his salvation is near those who fear him,
that his glory may dwell in our land.
Love and faithfulness meet together;
righteousness and peace kiss each other.
Faithfulness springs forth from the earth,
and righteousness looks down from heaven.
Righteousness goes before him
and prepares the way for his steps.

PSALM 85:8–11,13

The promised child

Then Isaiah said,
'Hear now, you house of David!
Is it not enough to try the patience of men?
Will you try the patience of my God also?
Therefore the Lord himself will give you a sign:
The virgin will be with child
and will give birth to a son,
and will call him Immanuel.'   ISAIAH 7:13,14

In those days Caesar Augustus issued a decree
that a census should be taken
     of the entire Roman world.
(This was the first census that took place
while Quirinius was governor of Syria.)
And everyone went to his own town to register.
So Joseph also went up
from the town of Nazareth in Galilee
to Judea, to Bethlehem the town of David,
because he belonged to the house and line of David.
He went there to register with Mary,
who was pledged to be married to him
and was expecting a child.
While they were there,
the time came for the baby to be born,
and she gave birth to her firstborn, a son.
She wrapped him in strips of cloth
and placed him in a manger,
because there was no room for them in the inn.
     LUKE 2:1–7

For you know the grace of our Lord Jesus Christ,
that though he was rich,
yet for your sakes he became poor,
so that you through his poverty might become rich.
     2 CORINTHIANS 8:9

Jesus is born

For to us a child is born, to us a son is given,
and the government will be on his shoulders.
And he will be called Wonderful Counsellor,
Mighty God, Everlasting Father, Prince of Peace.
Of the increase of his government and peace
there will be no end.
He will reign on David's throne and over his kingdom,
establishing and upholding it
with justice and righteousness
from that time on and for ever.   ISAIAH 9:6,7

And there were shepherds
living out in the fields nearby,
keeping watch over their flocks at night.
An angel of the Lord appeared to them,
and the glory of the Lord shone around them,
and they were terrified.
But the angel said to them,
'Do not be afraid.
I bring you good news of great joy
that will be for all the people.
Today in the town of David
a Saviour has been born to you;
he is Christ the Lord.
This will be a sign to you:
You will find a baby wrapped in strips of cloth
and lying in a manger.'
Suddenly a great company of the heavenly host
appeared with the angel,
praising God and saying,
'Glory to God in the highest,
and on earth peace to men
on whom his favour rests.'   LUKE 2:8–14

Rejoice in the Saviour!

The people walking in darkness
have seen a great light;
on those living in the land of the shadow of death
a light has dawned.
You have enlarged the nation and increased their joy. . .
For as in the day of Midian's defeat,
you have shattered the yoke that burdens them,
the bar across their shoulders,
the rod of their oppressor.　　　　　ISAIAH 9:2,3,4

When the angels had left them
and gone into heaven,
the shepherds said to one another,
'Let's go to Bethlehem
and see this thing that has happened,
which the Lord has told us about.'
So they hurried off
and found Mary and Joseph,
and the baby, who was lying in the manger.
When they had seen him,
they spread the word
concerning what had been told them about this child,
and all who heard it
were amazed at what the shepherds said to them.
But Mary treasured up all these things
and pondered them in her heart.
The shepherds returned,
glorifying and praising God
for all the things they had heard and seen,
which were just as they had been told.　　　　　LUKE 2:15–20

God sent his Son

This is how God showed his love among us:
He sent his one and only Son into the world
that we might live through him.
This is love: not that we loved God,
but that he loved us and sent his Son
as an atoning sacrifice for our sins.   1 JOHN 4:9,10

But when the time had fully come,
God sent his Son,
born of a woman,
born under law,
to redeem those under law,
that we might receive the full rights of sons.   GALATIANS 4:4,5

This is how the birth of Jesus Christ came about.
His mother Mary was pledged to be married to Joseph,
but before they came together,
she was found to be with child
through the Holy Spirit.
. . .An angel of the Lord
appeared to Joseph in a dream and said,
'Joseph son of David,
do not be afraid to take Mary home as your wife,
because what is conceived in her
is from the Holy Spirit.
She will give birth to a son,
and you are to give him the name Jesus,
because he will save his people from their sins.'
                                    MATTHEW 1:18,20,21

The servant

Who has believed our message
and to whom has the arm of the Lord been revealed?
He grew up before him like a tender shoot,
and like a root out of dry ground.
He had no beauty or majesty to attract us to him,
nothing in his appearance that we should desire him.
He was despised and rejected by men,
a man of sorrows, and familiar with suffering.
Like one from whom men hide their faces
he was despised, and we esteemed him not.   ISAIAH 53:1–3

The Word became flesh and lived for a while among us.
We have seen his glory,
the glory of the one and only Son,
who came from the Father,
full of grace and truth.
He was in the world,
and though the world was made through him,
the world did not recognise him.
He came to that which was his own,
but his own did not receive him.
Yet to all who received him,
to those who believed in his name,
he gave the right to become children of God.

JOHN 1:14,10–12

Christ Jesus . . . being in very nature God,
did not consider equality with God
something to be grasped,
but made himself nothing,
taking the very nature of a servant,
being made in human likeness.   PHILIPPIANS 2:5,6,7

He will rule his people

'But you, Bethlehem Ephrathah,
though you are small among the clans of Judah,
out of you will come for me
one who will be ruler over Israel,
whose origins are from of old, from ancient times.'
He will stand and shepherd his flock
in the strength of the Lord,
in the majesty of the name of the Lord his God.
And they will live securely, for then his greatness
will reach to the ends of the earth.
And he will be their peace. . .   MICAH 5:2,4

After Jesus was born in Bethlehem in Judea,
during the time of King Herod,
Magi from the east came to Jerusalem and asked,
'Where is the one who has been born king of the Jews?
We saw his star in the east
and have come to worship him.'
When King Herod heard this he was disturbed,
and all Jerusalem with him.
When he had called together
all the people's chief priests
and teachers of the law,
he asked them where the Christ was to be born.
'In Bethlehem in Judea,' they replied,
'for this is what the prophet has written.'   MATTHEW 2:1–5

Christ – God's truth and glory

In the past
God spoke to our forefathers through the prophets
at many times and in various ways,
but in these last days
he has spoken to us by his Son,
whom he appointed heir of all things,
and through whom he made the universe.
The Son is the radiance of God's glory
and the exact representation of his being,
sustaining all things by his powerful word.
After he had provided purification for sins,
he sat down at the right hand
    of the Majesty in heaven.   HEBREWS 1:1–3

Concerning this salvation,
the prophets,
who spoke of the grace that was to come to you,
searched intently and with the greatest care,
trying to find out the time and circumstances
to which the Spirit of Christ in them was pointing
when he predicted the sufferings of Christ
and the glories that would follow.   1 PETER 1:10,11

Christ – God's living Word

In the beginning was the Word,
and the Word was with God,
and the Word was God.
He was with God in the beginning.
Through him all things were made;
without him nothing was made that has been made.
In him was life,
and that life was the light of men.
The light shines in the darkness,
but the darkness has not understood it.
There came a man who was sent from God;
his name was John.
He came as a witness
to testify concerning that light,
so that through him all men might believe.
He himself was not the light;
he came only as a witness to the light.
The true light that gives light to every man
was coming into the world.
John testifies concerning him.
He cries out, saying,
'This was he of whom I said,
"He who comes after me has surpassed me
because he was before me." '
From the fullness of his grace
we have all received one blessing after another.
For the law was given through Moses:
grace and truth came through Jesus Christ.

JOHN 1:1–9,15–17